# CHOOSING HAPPINESS

## *Working Within*

FRANCISCO UGARTE

Scepter

While every effort has been made to obtain existing accepted English translation or the English original of quoted text, some quotes have been translated by Scepter Publishers in the instance of no accepted English equivalent having been found.



Published by Scepter Publishers, Inc.
info@scepterpublishers.org
www.scepterpublishers.org
800-322-8773
New York



Text and cover by Rose Design



Printed in the United States of America

Library of Congress Cataloging-in-Publication Data

Names: Ugarte Corcuera, Francisco, author.
Title: Choosing happiness : working within / Francisco Ugarte.
Other titles: Camino de la felicidad. English
Description: New York : Scepter Publishers, 2016.
Identifiers: LCCN 2016046445 | ISBN 9781594172625 (pbk.)
Subjects: LCSH: Happiness. | Happiness—Religious aspects—Christianity.
Classification: LCC BF575.H27 U3313 2016 | DDC 152.4/2—dc23
LC record available at https://lccn.loc.gov/2016046445

ISBN: book 978-1-59417-262-5
ISBN: ebook 978-1-59417-263-2

# Contents

# Introduction

Reflecting on the subject of happiness is fascinating because we all aspire to be happy. We desire the same for those we love; we always want the best for them.

In the literature about happiness, which is surprisingly scarce for a subject of such importance, we tend to find two approaches: the classic and the contemporary. The classic approach, which explains the nature of happiness philosophically, may seem rather abstract to the modern reader, who seeks practical solutions relating to everyday life. The contemporary approach, however, is often reduced to "formulas" for making us happy, formulas that don't solve the basic problem because they lack content.

The purpose of this book is to delve more deeply into the substance of happiness, to reveal the way to be happy in daily life, and to connect this daily joy with the infinite happiness of the next life. As the title

*Choosing Happiness: Working Within* suggests, it's a matter of looking inside ourselves and at our truest, deepest needs, choosing to be happy in this life and the next by identifying and seeking those sources of happiness which meet and match authentic human needs.

It's not enough to *want* to be happy; we have to *learn how* to be so. Otherwise we run the risk of failing to grasp what is truly involved in this conquest. Learning how to be happy means:

- determining where happiness exists (and where it does not) in order to head in the right direction;
- avoiding the obstacles—especially internal ones, such as resentment—and eliminating them if they are present;
- recognizing the attitudes and dispositions that promote happiness—such as gratitude and optimism—and how we can cultivate these with practice;
- taking responsibility for our own happiness, given that it's not a matter of chance or good luck;

- choosing to be happy in the course of ordinary life rather than waiting to find joy in results or extraordinary moments;
- discovering how to rise above difficult and painful situations so that they are integrated into the meaning of life itself and do not destroy happiness.

The ideas offered in this book reflect an attempt to capture the essence of happiness and how to attain it. They have been shared with people whose circumstances and ways of thinking are quite diverse and whose feedback and input have contributed decisively to this work. My principal desire is that those who read these pages will discover insights that can help them in *Choosing Happiness*.

1

CHAPTER

# I Want to Be Happy!

## The Natural Inclination toward Happiness

We all want to be happy. It's difficult to refute this, especially if we interpret the verb *want* as both desire and seek. Who wants unhappiness? Who does not use the pursuit of happiness as the very basis for all actions? The child who enters a toy store is not merely seeking a toy, but happiness; the student who works toward a college degree to obtain success in the work force is not seeking fame, but happiness; the researcher who endeavors to unlock some mystery is not seeking knowledge alone, but happiness. Therefore, the worst circumstance that can happen to any of us is not to properly resolve our inclinations toward happiness. In this vein, the Argentinean author Jorge Luis Borges writes in one of his poems:

> I have committed the worst sin of all
> That a man can commit. I have not been
> Happy. Let the glaciers of oblivion
> Drag me and mercilessly let me fall.
> My parents bred and bore me for
> a higher
> Faith in the human game of nights
> and days;
> For earth, for air, for water, and for fire.
> I let them down. I wasn't happy."[1]

The fact is that we are made for happiness. For that reason, we naturally tend toward it, drawn by the same innate force that makes stones fall. Only in humans, this instinctive inclination is paradoxically free: we cannot want anything other than to be happy and,

---

1. Jorge Luis Borges, "Remorse," *Six Masters of the Spanish Sonnet*, trans. Willis Barnstone (Carbondale, IL: Southern Illinois University Press, 1993), p. 223.

at the same time, we want it freely. Thomas Aquinas pointed this out when he wrote that to "say that the will necessarily wills something, such as happiness, is not contrary to the freedom of the will."[2] But we can object that certain human actions seem to work directly against the happiness of the person who does them, such as damaging the body by using drugs, harming a loved one, or simply isolating oneself from others in order to immerse in sorrow. Are these exceptions to that universal desire for happiness?

Pascal emphatically says "No," even when referring to the most extreme act of suicide. "All men seek happiness. This is without exception. Whatever different means they employ, they all tend to this end. . . . This is the motive of every action of every man, even of those who hang themselves."[3]

It can be a challenge to ensure that, in practice, the subjective desire of being happy (which is always present) is resolved

---

2. Thomas Aquinas, *De Potentia* 10.2.5 in *The Power of God*, trans. Richard J. Regan, (Oxford, NY: Oxford University Press, 2012).

3. Blaise Pascal, "Morality And Doctrine," *Pensées*, trans. W. F. Trotter (Mineola, NY: Dover, 2003), 7.425.

satisfactorily. St. Augustine observed that although men wish to be happy, they don't really know how to attain happiness.[4] Therefore, it is one thing to desire to be happy and another to actually be so. When we experience severe difficulty in experiencing happiness, what usually happens is that we speak of the impossibility of being happy as something inherent in the human condition. Such is the conception of the radical existentialists. "Both the 'Nazi' Heidegger and the leftist Sartre shared an existential outlook marked by anxiety, if not by depression: man is a 'being for death,' a useless passion. The notion of happiness seems to them—and to many others—a trivial, dishonest, elusive term."[5]

If we consider personal experience, however, we will surely find the most convincing confirmation of the opening line of this chapter: "We all want to be happy," although we know intuitively that it will not be easy to accomplish.

---

4. Augustine, *Expositions on the Psalms, Vol. V* 118.1.1.

5. Fernando Savater, "Prólogo," in Russell Bertrand's *La conquista de la felicidad*, (Debolsillo, Barcelona, 2004), p. 9.

## Pleasure, Joy, and Happiness

The path to happiness seems to be progressive in the sense that we can never say, while traveling it, that we have reached the goal. We can always be happier. And being happy is equivalent to having "a successful life," as various contemporary authors have rightly noted;[6] the subjective consequence of happiness is a sensation of permanent peace, which can be distinguished from simple pleasure and also from joy.

C.S. Lewis illustrates these differences with a sad personal experience that occurred when he was still a boy. "With my mother's death all settled happiness, all that was tranquil and reliable, disappeared from my life. There was to be much fun, many pleasures, many stabs of Joy; but no more of the old security. It was sea and islands now; the great continent had sunk like Atlantis."[7] His

---

6. See Robert Spaemann, *Happiness and Benevolence*, trans. J. Alberg (Edinburgh: T & T Clark, 2000); Alejandro Llano, *La vida lograda* (Barcelona: Ariel, 2002).

7. C.S. Lewis, *Surprised by Joy: The Shape of My Early Life* (Orlando: Harcourt Brace & Co., 1955), p. 21.

experience supports Aristotle's claim that happiness should be something stable.[8]

Whenever we attain or possess a good, we experience a favorable emotion that might be referred to as *pleasure*. In philosophical language, this is understood as *relaxing in the possession of a good*. This state can later give way to three distinct situations: If the good is something material, what we experience is sensible pleasure, which is ordinarily characterized by transience, a lack of permanence. If the good in question is more important and at the same time something concrete—love for a person, for example—or if it refers to a particular accomplishment, such as having finished a college career—the pleasure we experience is called *joy*. Bergson emphasizes, "Joy always announces that life has succeeded, gained ground, conquered."[9] In contrast, if the joy proceeds not from a

8. See Aristotle, *Nicomachean Ethics* 1, in Aristotle, *Nicomachean Ethics*, trans. Roger Crisp (UK: Cambridge University Press, 2000).

9. Henri Bergson, as quoted in *Understanding Bergson, Understanding Modernism*, eds. Paul Ardoin, S. E. Gontarski, and Laci Mattison (New York: Bloomsbury, 2013), p. 123.

particular circumstance, but from our integral life situations, it has a permanent character that we properly call *happiness.*

In sum, "Joy is above pleasure and below happiness. Pleasure has a fleeting, transient, elusive tone; it is important, and it opens a window of fresh air. But joy has a more enduring tone and presents itself as a consequence of having attained something through personal effort and struggle. On another level, on another galaxy, we find ourselves with happiness: the sum and compendium of an authentic life and of seeing the 'project' afloat."[10] It consists, then, in the joy that proceeds, not from a particular good or circumstance, but from everyday life. "Happiness is a condition of the person himself, of one's whole self; that is to say it is in the order of being, and not of having."[11] It is deeper and more permanent than joy or pleasure.

---

10. Enrique Rojas, *Una teoría de la felicidad* (Madrid: Dossat 2000), p. 8.

11. Ricardo Yepes Stork, *Fundamentos de antropologia* (Pamplona: EUNSA, 1996), p. 216.

Nevertheless, some thinkers are not in accord with this triple distinction because they possess a reductionist conception of happiness. They identify happiness with pleasure alone, like John Stuart Mill, principal representative of the utilitarian school. Mill asserts, "By happiness is intended pleasure, and the absence of pain; by unhappiness, pain, and the privation of pleasure."[12] We must note that, for this author, pleasure is not reduced to mere sensible pleasure, that proper to animals; rather, it includes that which corresponds to the superior faculties of the human person.[13]

The three distinctions described here correspond to a state of being that we often colloquially refer to as *happiness.* We say that someone is *happy* when we are actually referring to the immediate result of a specific pleasant stimulus, such as alcohol; we

---

12. John Stuart Mill, *Utilitarianism, 2nd ed.*, ed. George Sher (Indianapolis: Hackett, 2001), p. 7.

13. "A beast's pleasures do not satisfy a human being's conceptions of happiness. Human beings have faculties more elevated than the animal appetites and, when once made conscious of them, do not regard anything as happiness which does not include their gratification." Mill, *Utilitarianism*, p. 8.

say someone is *happy* when a life event produces a perception of more stable happiness, such as attaining a goal. The latter is more properly identified with *joy*; we can say that we *are joyful* for having achieved what we have intentionally worked toward. It is one's *permanent* situation, one that no longer depends on particular circumstances, that constitutes *happiness*.

## The Insufficiency of Pleasure

Today, people seem obsessed with seeking material well-being, comfort, and all that produces sensible and sensual pleasure. We find ourselves very much conditioned—not determined—by a vast array of propaganda using highly refined techniques to keep us on a quest for what is pleasurable, as though that is the ultimate possession, the supreme source of happiness, which also includes the rejection of suffering. As Julián Marías expressed it, "One has to seek the happiness of the greatest number, the greatest quantity of pleasure and the minimum amount of suffering, and that the sufferings be transitory and pass by quickly. This is close to the general opinion of the present-day world."[14]

This attitude is not new. The Roman poet, Horace, coined the term "*carpe diem*," meaning "seize the day," take advantage of the moment, don't miss the opportunity, and live in the present. This perspective identifies happiness with immediate pleasure and invites us to ignore the future, which surely will bring with it complications: work, old age, lack of money, sickness, and death. What we have to do is enjoy the now—and as much as possible. We must be rooted in the present: *carpe diem!*[15] Although this attitude is not new, who can dispute that this mode of thinking has grown increasingly powerful in today's world? Therefore, we urgently need to determine whether pleasure can satisfy the desire to be happy.

Without falling into the extreme of the Stoics, who considered pleasure something necessarily bad and contrary to human

---

14. Marías, Julian, *La Felicidad humana*, (Madrid: Alianza Editorial, 2005), p. 234.

15. See Yepes Stork, p. 230.

nature—Seneca held that "pleasure is something low, slavish, weak, decrepit, whose place and home are the brothels and taverns"[16]—we can recognize that sensible pleasure, even when it is licit and good, is transitory; it doesn't last long. Happiness, in contrast, is lasting. Pleasure, because of its transitory nature, its fleetingness, cannot resolve the problem of happiness. Those who center their lives on sensible joy will experience the distressing ease with which pleasure escapes their hands; they want the satisfactions derived from pleasant moments to last, but they end. The consequence of placing our hopes in pleasure is an inner vacuum that frustrates us if we try to be happy on this path; we end up more dissatisfied than we were before the pleasant experience.

There are physiological reasons why pleasure fails to fulfill or satisfy as a source of happiness when we seek it as an end in itself. If we hold an obsessive inclination toward

---

16. Seneca, *De vita beata 7.3*, as quoted in David Fredrick, ed., *The Roman Gaze: Vision, Power, and the Body*, (Baltimore: The Johns Hopkins University Press, 2002), p. 91.

pleasure, we tend to return, again and again, to the stimuli that produced the desired pleasant sensations. The effect is that our capacity to enjoy the pleasure, to take delight in those stimuli, begins to decline in direct proportion to the frequency and intensity of exposure. The pleasant sensation proceeding from the same stimulus becomes less and less. The result, if we were to persist in seeking pleasure at any cost, is that we would need to find stronger stimulants to make up for this loss of desired sensation. A very clear example of this exists with drugs and sex. With drugs, a person who begins with less harmful "soft drugs" must move on to stronger ones because the pleasure derived from the first declines. In the case of sex, an individual carried along by instinct in trying to satisfy a lustful appetite egotistically is never satisfied; the person begins to seek a wider range of experiences. The inevitable result is a lack of sexual satisfaction originating from the mistaken focus of this activity, which has been exclusively on pleasure.

Therefore, we see that the life of a person who is centered on pleasure will spiral into absurdity and contradiction. Humans were not made to spend life steeped in pleasant experiences; we are called to project our lives toward ideals that are higher than those provided by the senses. This is why Viktor Frankl asserted, "If pleasure was really the meaning of life, one would have to come to the conclusion that life really lacks any meaning."[17]

## Well-Being and Quality of Life

Pleasure can also be viewed as the goal of human life in a more subtle way, under the guise of *well-being*. Understood as the assemblage of basic material conditions that permit us to lead lives that are truly human, well-being needs no justification. But when well-being becomes the central objective of life and is identified largely with material comforts, it is usually accompanied by the renunciation of higher values, those of the immaterial and spiritual order. Therefore, we can understand why a European leader,

17. Viktor Frankl, *Psicoanálisis y existencialismo* (Mexico City: Fondo de Cultura Economica, Breviario 27, 1967), p. 52.

when asked about the situation of his fellow citizens, believed that his countrymen were *dying of comfort.*[18] For the fact is that material well-being, poorly understood, can become an agonizing breeding ground in which human life becomes insufferable, despite the comforts that surround it. In any case, "well-being by itself does not produce happiness; it is simply a requisite for it. Happiness does not consist simply in being comfortable, but in doing something that fills one's life."[19]

These days, we use the expression "quality of life," which conveys the contemporary understanding of well-being. It includes the following aspects:

- maintaining physical and mental health (care of the mind and body);
- ensuring contact with nature and eliminating contaminated environments;
- taking advantage of the means that technology offers to meet material and

18. He refers here to Guy Debord, a French theorist, writer, filmmaker, and founding member of the Situationist International.

19. Marías, p. 170.

personal needs; availing oneself of technological advances that fill life with comforts and make it increasingly pleasant.

While each of these aspects, taken in isolation, can hold a particular value, their focus as a whole is negative, in that it is rooted in the inability of any material object to enrich human life in an integral way. Here everything seems to be centered, indeed, on well-being but without opening our perspective to the goods and values that give substance to our humanity and lead us to successful lives. *Quality of life*, therefore is not sufficient to attain the plenitude that happiness implies.

In the face of the insufficiency of pleasure and well-being, it seems necessary to orient our lives toward higher values, which will require the best of us, drawing on our strengths through acts that evoke feelings of satisfaction more than of pleasure. Martin Seligman notes, "The 'pleasant life' might be had by drinking champagne and driving a Porsche, but not the good life. Rather, the good life is using your signature strengths every day to produce authentic happiness and abundant gratification. This is something you can learn to do in each of the main realms of your life: work, love, and raising children."[20]

## A Difficult Conquest

Because happiness is a matter of profound reality, which can be reduced neither to pleasure nor to simple joy, we should expect that the conquest of happiness is not easy. The Roman philosopher Seneca noted that "all men . . . wish to live happily, but are dull at perceiving exactly what it is that makes life happy: and so far is it from being easy to attain to happiness that the more eagerly a man struggles to reach it the further he departs from it. . . ."[21]

The pessimist Schopenhauer claimed that to live happily only meant to live the least unhappily as possible, to live in an endurable

---

20. Martin E. P. Seligman, *Authentic Happiness* (Toronto: The Free Press, 2002), p. 13.

21. Seneca, *Minor Dialogues: Together with the Dialogue on Clemency*, trans. Aubrey Stewart (London: George Bell and Sons, 1898), p. 204.

way.[22] Thus many, not finding an answer to what we most desire, end up renouncing happiness or avoiding the problem.

"Don't we avoid using the word 'happiness'? Don't we use it timidly, almost with shame, as if it belonged to the lexicon of the enthusiasms of youth, that is, of those illusions which the mature, reasonable man no longer has the right to maintain?"[23] It is also significant that today, "for every one hundred journal articles on sadness, there is just one on happiness."[24] This leads us to think that we are very much in need of a culture that tells us how to be happy.

Nevertheless, "the tragedy of man is not that of not being able to find happiness, but of seeking it where it is not."[25] We sometimes try to satisfy our anxiety over happiness by acquiring sensible goods, which provide only

---

22. Bryan Magee, *The Philosophy of Schopenhauer* (New York: Oxford University Press, 1983), p. 241.

23. Giovanni Reale, *La sabiduria antigua* (Barcelona: Herder, 1996), 95.

24. Seligman, p. 6.

25. Walter Farrell and Martin J. Healy, *My Way of Life: The Summa Simplified for Everyone* (Brooklyn, NY: Confraternity of the Precious Blood, 1952), 191.

transitory pleasures, or through particular situations that offer only partial joys. If we really want to find the deep happiness that proceeds from having a *successful life*, we must learn where this can be found so that we can go out and acquire it.

Aristotle himself spoke of the difficulty of reaching an agreement on this question, stating that the masses and the learned explain the essence of happiness in two different ways: "For the masses think it is something straightforward and obvious, like pleasure, wealth, or honour. . . . Often the same person can give different accounts: when he is ill, it is health; when he is poor, it is wealth. And when people are aware of their ignorance, they marvel at those who say it is some grand thing quite beyond them. Certain thinkers used to believe that beyond these many good things there is something else good in itself, which makes all these good things good."[26]

In the process of getting close to true happiness, in both theory and practice, it is necessary to understand that because the

26. Aristotle, *Nicomachean Ethics* 1.4.109.5a in Crisp, pp. 5–6.

concept is complex, we cannot simplify it and come up with some kind of cheap formula that provides the solution. Bossuet said, "Happiness is made up of so many pieces that there is always one missing."[27] Although this statement may sound ultimately pessimistic, it is worthwhile to consider the first part, because it states a great truth. The conquest of happiness consists in discovering and harmoniously integrating those multiple pieces that constitute it. One characteristic is common to all of the pieces that must be present in order to bring about happiness: the quality or perfection with which they have been constructed.

We have seen that everyone is inclined toward happiness and that, at the same time, finding it is a difficult task. Is it really possible to be happy? The negative answers to this question go from the constitutive impossibility for happiness in man held by radical existentialism to the skepticism of Fernando Savater in our time, who asserts: "As far as

27. Jacques-Bénigne Bossuet, quoted in Georges Chevrot, *Las Bienaventuranzas* (Madrid: Rialp, 1987), pp. 32–33.

conquering happiness, happiness properly understood . . . on this I do not have too many illusions."[28] Theologically speaking, one negative focus places the possibility of being happy in the next life, after death, as though being unhappy now were a prerequisite for meriting future happiness. Let us consider this last idea.

Some people conceive of happiness in this life as counterpoised to the happiness of heaven: either we are happy here or we are happy there. Those of us who want to attain definitive happiness should resign ourselves to being unhappy now; it is the price we must pay to merit eternal happiness. This outlook leads to resignation in the face of a life that is necessarily unhappy.

One who has faith knows that human beings have a "natural desire for happiness. This desire is of divine origin. God has placed it in the human heart in order to draw man to the One who alone can fulfill it."[29] God

28. Savater, p. 13.

29. *Catechism of the Catholic Church* (2nd ed.) (Washington, DC: Libreria Editrice Vaticana–United States Conference of Catholic Bishops, 2000), 1718.

absolutely wants us to experience happiness and desires that we freely accept his offer of help to attain it. But where does one find the happiness that God wants one to attain: in this life or only in life after death? Is there any relationship between being happy now and being happy afterward?

## Is Happiness for This Life or the Next?

St. Josemaría Escrivá pointed out that "our Lord does not expect us to be unhappy in our life on earth and await a reward only in the next life. God wants us to be happy on earth, too, but with a desire for the other, total happiness that only he can give."[30] Even more, St. Josemaría could affirm that "'happiness in heaven is for those who know how to be happy on earth."[31] In this approach, obviously, there is no room for mere passive resignation to a life with problems and difficulties; rather, life becomes an active search for that happiness for which God has created us.

---

30. Josemaría Escrivá, *Christ Is Passing By* (New York: Scepter, 2002), 126.

31. Josemaría Escrivá, *The Forge* (New York: Scepter, 2011), 1005.

But another question could arise: Is this perspective compatible with pain and suffering; could it not be that the misfortunes and tragedies of life are the price to pay to gain heaven? The way Jesus proceeded, as depicted in so many Gospel scenes, provides an answer to these questions. "God wants the happiness of men here on earth as in heaven. It is false that he makes us purchase future happiness at the cost of the evils of the present. Open the Gospel. Did he remain indifferent to the sufferings of men? Did he not sympathize with the pain of the sisters of Lazarus before their brother's tomb, to such an extent that he himself wept? If our present evils were the condition of our future happiness, would Jesus have cured so many crippled and so many sick people, depriving them in this hypothesis of their surest possibility of being happy?"[32] Therefore, although God permits the pain and suffering of men and women as an opportunity for meriting eternal life, he also wants us to learn to bear those evils in a way that does not convert us

32. Chevrot, p. 32.

into people without joy. On the contrary, and paradoxically, he permits even sorrows and evils to be a part of the path of happiness in this life as well.

The practical consequences of these two focuses are very clear. On the one hand, if we consider that being unhappy now is the condition for being happy later, we will live with a negative attitude that will hinder our enjoyment of the goods that God himself has given us. We will be inclined to renounce licit pleasures and valid joys, to open ourselves unilaterally to all that brings suffering, sadness, or bitterness. It would be difficult to live such a life with intensity; most likely, such an approach would not permit one's talents to bear fruit, forecasting a life that would end in frustration.

On the other hand, if we discover the close connection and continuity between present and future happiness, we will adopt a positive attitude, one that will lead us to learn to be happy now in order to attain eternal life later. Among other benefits, we will live with gratitude to God and our fellow man for the gifts that we receive, and we will try to do as much good as possible so that our talents bear the maximum fruit. This way of life will serve as a basic source of satisfaction here and preparation for definitive happiness. Problems, pain, and suffering, when they appear, will be accepted, and we will try to discover their meaning so that we can turn them into sources of happiness, although this requires a special learning process. Because of the importance of suffering in relation to happiness, we will delve more deeply into this subject in the final chapter. For right now, we must focus on answering the following questions: How do we attain happiness in this life? Where do we find it? What is the path to attaining it?

2

CHAPTER

# Where is Happiness Found?

The great majority of people seek happiness in pleasure and in material things. This assertion has already been explained with some care because pleasure cannot fulfill the yearning for happiness that lies hidden within each of us. We will now analyze whether material things could be the answer to the yearning for happiness. If that is not the case, we will need to seek some other source that better corresponds to the structure of the human person.

## The Possession of Material Goods

Human life, in order to be lived with dignity and attain the development that corresponds to it, requires material means. This does not mean that any direct proportion exists between the quantity of those goods and the degree of happiness obtainable through them. Experience has shown that the accumulation of money, of riches, does not make people happy. And it is not infrequently that we encounter the paradox that the more we have, the more unhappy we become, as has been shown by serious studies in developed countries.[1] "While real income in America has risen 16 percent in the last thirty years, the percentage of people who describe themselves as 'very happy' has fallen from 36 to

---

1. "A paradox rules our lives. Most people want to increase their income and struggle to do this, but although Western societies have become richer, the people who live in them are not happier. This is not an old folktale; it is a fact demonstrated by works of scientific research. . . . We have trustworthy means of measuring people's happiness, and all the evidence points out that, in general, people are not happier than they were fifty years ago, even though median incomes have doubled or increased even more. This paradox is equally valid for the United States, Great Britain, and Japan." Richard Layard, *La felicidad, Lecciones de una nueva ciencia* (Mexico City: Taurus, 2005), 15.

29 percent."[2] Those who struggle to attain a relatively important position in life based on financial success, thinking wealth will make them happy, feel themselves deceived. And the fact is that *having* material goods does not satisfy the desires for happiness that are hidden in the heart of man.[3] Why is this the case?

When we live for material goods, to accumulate riches, *the more we have, the more we want.* The appetite grows, progressively, as our possessions grow, to an infinite degree, as Thomas Aquinas noted: "The desire for artificial wealth is infinite."[4] A vicious circle is generated that makes satisfying our desires impossible. The greater the possessions, the greater the appetite; the greater the appetite, the greater the quest for material goods, and the cycle continues. As a result, desire moves

---

2. Seligman.

3. "When all men have all that they desire, there is still a lot needed to be happy. The Western world shows that it is then when they are least happy, because it is then that their problems begin. Therefore the salvation of man is not a thing of bread and money. He has a hunger for something more. The refuge in drugs, which today is a massive phenomenon, shows this very clearly. Man needs meaning no less than bread." Joseph Ratzinger, *Palabra en la Iglesia* (Salamanca: Sigueme, 1976), 196.

4. Aquinas, *Summa Theologica* 1–2.2.1.

further and further from the goods already obtained, and accordingly, dissatisfaction becomes more acute. The distance between ambition and the goods possessed is ordinarily greater in those who have more. And if those who have more are attached to what they possess, the relationship is the same, with the consequent unhappiness. Therefore this saying, which is attributed to St. Francis of Assisi, is full of wisdom: "I desire little, and what little I desire, I desire little."

From another point of view, we can also understand why material goods cannot provide happiness. This is simply because the deepest needs that we must satisfy in order to be happy are not of a material order but are *immaterial.* Money and riches, in general, cannot supply our need for affection, nor our eagerness to know the truth that lurks in the depths of every human mind. The higher potencies of our humanity, such as intellect, will, and affectivity, grow and develop by means of another kind of reality of a non-material character, one that offers better guarantees of permanence. There is a significant distinction between those goods that encourage us to *be more* and the accumulation of material objects, which fosters the quest to *have more*. The well-known Mexican writer Octavio Paz says, "Our time . . . is simplistic, superficial, and merciless. Having fallen into the idolatry of ideological systems, our century has ended by worshiping *things*. What place does love have in such a world?"[5]

"Whoever said money can't buy happiness isn't spending it right," declares an advertisement for Lexus cars. Yet there is a reason why money and riches cannot be the source of happiness, for happiness consists of a deeper character, and Aristotle points to it: "Happiness in particular is believed to be complete without qualification, since we always choose it for itself and never for the sake of anything else."[6] Other things we desire as a cause of happiness. For this reason, "wealth is clearly not the good we are seeking, since it is merely useful, for getting something else."[7]

---

5. Octavio Paz, *The Double Flame: Love and Eroticism*, trans. Helen Lane (New York: Harcourt Brace & Company, 1995), p. 186.

6. Aristotle, *Nicomachean Ethics* 1.7.1097b in Crisp, pp. 10–11.

7. Aristotle, *Nicomachean Ethics* 1.5.1096a in Crisp, p. 7.

The conclusion is, therefore, clear: material goods lack sufficient importance to resolve the problem of human happiness.

## An Interior Task

Is there any way to measure happiness that will provide definitive results or conclusions? An increasing number of experimental studies have attempted to measure happiness through tests or interviews. We might argue that these studies, based on statistics, do not clarify much nor delve deeply enough into the qualitative aspect of happiness; they are reduced to a review of what people understand as "being or feeling happy," without detailing the content of happiness itself. Nevertheless, despite their limitations in regard to obtaining definitive conclusions, these procedures are valuable, inasmuch as they are based on people's concrete experiences. If complemented by adequate philosophical reflection, they can offer interesting and valuable insights.

Often these results confirm what philosophy contends. For example, a study by David G. Myers (Hope College, Michigan) and Ed

Diener (University of Illinois), carried out over a period of more than ten years,[8] showed the following:

- Married people tend to be happier than those who are single.
- People who increase their income over a ten-year period are not happier than those who do not increase it.
- Believers with a spiritual commitment are happier than the indifferent, and happiness increases in parallel with one's religious practice.

The most valuable result of the investigation, in my judgment, was its principal conclusion that "happiness does not appear to depend significantly on external circumstances."[9] This finding is of great value because it illuminates the path for seeking happiness where it can truly be found. It confirms what a healthy philosophical anthropology points out: "The deepest and most

---

8. See David G. Myers and Ed Diener, "The Pursuit of Happiness," *Scientific American*, May 1996, pp. 54–56.

9. Myers and Diener, p. 54.

elevated facets of man are found in his interior. We seek happiness in vain exteriorly if we don't find it within ourselves; human fullness bears within itself riches of spirit, peace and harmony of soul, serenity. *The path of happiness is within us:* it is an interior path."[10]

Such a conclusion contrasts with the paths that many people take in attempt to resolve their anxiety over happiness, paths which are entirely exterior: sensible pleasure, the possession of material goods, the esteem of others, success, physical appearance, power, and fame. In contrast, if we do not lose sight of the fact that "happiness is an inside job,"[11] it will be possible to advance in its study, centering our attention on the interior of our humanity and on those goods that can satisfy our deepest needs.

## Dependence on Choice

If happiness occurs in the interior of a human and if that is where we must work to obtain it,

10. Yepes Stork, p. 215.

11. John Powell, *Happiness Is an Inside Job* (Allen, TX: Tabor, 1989), p. 15.

it follows that our happiness depends on ourselves. Some who are not happy blame their unhappiness on another person—a husband, a mother-in-law, an associate at work—or on external circumstances, such as the economic situation, sickness, old age, the problems of the country, and so on. This makes it appear that to obtain happiness, we first must solve all of those difficulties, which may lead us to conclude that happiness is utopia and it is better to give up on it.

We may also be tempted to adopt a skeptical and timid attitude in order to avoid choosing happiness, trying to remain in a rather neutral state. Some people tend to retreat from the goal of happiness: they don't even dare to try to be happy. In this case, they may arrive at the end of life never having truly lived. This is what has been called the "temptation of Limbo."[12]

When we discover that happiness depends on ourselves—on the interior attitudes with which we confront the various successes and circumstances of life, the meaning assigned

12. Marías, 267.

to each, and how these attitudes affect our experience of life—our focus changes radically. When external factors exist but are no longer permitted to exert supreme influence, we realize that the solution lies within—and from that moment on, we may embrace a process that can offer a real solution. We can then decide to choose firmly for our own happiness and determine to employ the necessary means—principally internal—of attaining it.

Abraham Lincoln has been widely credited for stating that people are usually as happy as they make up their minds to be. Various philosophers with positive outlooks as well have proposed to show the way, as Bertrand Russell notes in the preface to his essay on happiness: "It is in the belief that many people who are unhappy could become happy by well-directed effort that I have written this book."[13]

It depends on each of us, therefore, to discern and savor the meaning that reality offers.

---

13. Bertrand Russell, *The Conquest of Happiness* (Oxfordshire: Routledge Classics, 2006), xiii.

The Spanish-Mexican philosopher Eduardo Nicol asked himself: "Could it not be that things become insipid when we lack the love with which they can be made to come alive? The tediousness of life, fastidiousness, or even the disgust that Sartre speaks of, could this not be a mirror of their own lives: the tediousness, the fastidiousness, and the disgust of those past and contemporary existentialists?"[14] In contrast, John Powell shared that, in order not to fall into the trap of waiting for happiness to come to him, he deliberately placed a memo on his bathroom mirror. Each day, the memo served to remind him that the face he saw in the mirror—his own—was that of the person responsible for his happiness.[15]

## What to Choose?

The idea that happiness depends on a personal choice means that the decision falls on us, and it involves varied aspects of our

---

14. Eduardo Nicol, *Las ideas y los dias* (Mexico City: Afinita, 2007), p. 198.

15. Powell.

behavior, our lives, and our beings. I will point out a few of these here.

1) *Choose attitudes that favor happiness.* For example, if we want to be optimistic, we must decide to look at the positive side of things before the negative. This determines whether we see the glass as "half full" or "half empty"; we decide what we want to see. We must also decide to notice the beauty in what is closest to us, so as to prevent what the Bengali poet Rabindranath Tagore observed with surprise, "For many years / without sparing the cost / I visited many countries, / I saw the highest mountains / and the oceans. / The only thing that I missed seeing was the sparkling of the dew on the grass at the door of my house."

2) *Watch our reactions.* We are in command of the way we react to the events that happen around us. Happiness "is not subordinate to the course that events take, but to the ways in which we react before them. Happiness depends on us; its source resides in ourselves."[16] Our reactions have a lot to do with

16. Chevrot, p. 31.

how we judge. For example, after a negative event, if we judge wisely and accept the error and the possibility of rectifying it, we will be happier. If on the other hand, we see ourselves as guilty but without any possibility of rectification, we distance ourselves from happiness.[17] As the Spanish researcher José Antonio Marina says, "There are personalities that seem poorly gifted for happiness because in every bump, they see a precipice and in every disappointment, a tragedy."[18] That is, they are not capable of reacting positively to problems. The solution in these cases consists in changing those negative feelings by means of a deliberate decision.

**3)** *Avoid egocentric orientation.* Kierkegaard's maxim rings true: *the door to happiness opens outward*, toward others. Hence, we have to "aim at avoiding self-centered passions and at

---

17. "Happiness does not depend on how many bad things happen to an individual. What is more important is whether an individual tends to make negative conclusions about him- or herself when negative events occur." Panos, 1997, quoted in David Niven, *The 100 Simple Secrets of Happy People* (San Francisco: Harper, 2000), p. 93.

18. José Antonio Marina, *El laberinto sentimental* (Barcelona: Anagrama, 1997), 208.

acquiring those affections and those interests which will prevent our thoughts from dwelling perpetually upon ourselves. It is not the nature of most men to be happy in a prison, and the passions which shut us up in ourselves constitute one of the worst kinds of prisons."[19] The opposite of egocentrism consists in getting out of oneself, giving oneself to others. "Only *in love* does man, with his final perfection specified and fully human, find his most radical happiness."[20]

4) *Orient our lives toward gratifications rather than sensible pleasures.* This is necessary, according to Seligman's terminology of Seligman, because "the *pleasures* are delights that have clear sensory and strong emotional components. . . . They are evanescent, and they involve little, if any, thinking."[21] In contrast, "Gratifications engage us fully, we become immersed and absorbed in them, and we lose self-consciousness. Enjoying a great conversation, rock climbing, reading a good

19. Russell, 171.

20. Tomás Melendo, *El "efecto" felicidad* (Mexico City: Trillas, 2008), p. 84.

21. Seligman, 102.

book, dancing, and making a slam dunk are all examples of activities in which time stops for us, our skills match the challenge, and we are in touch with our strengths. The gratifications last longer than the pleasures, they involve quite a lot of thinking and interpretation . . . and they are undergirded by our strengths and virtues."[22]

5) *We, ourselves, have to make the decision.* This means, on a more profound level, that such an option has to mark the path that leads us toward plenitude, toward the success that is a consequence of orienting life in accord with the truth of the person, so that we are giving the best of ourselves. Here it is a matter of making a choice for the permanent growth of our being, which translates into *being more*, progressively, from which happiness derives.

Complementary to this, the option for happiness must take into account that it is a long-term process, one that is not accomplished with a single blow but through a gradual process that lasts a lifetime. "We have

---

22. Seligman, 102.

to take into account that we are not born happy or unhappy but that we learn to be the one or the other; to a great extent, whether we reach happiness or misfortune depends on the choices we make. It is not true, as many people believe, that happiness can be found as one finds a coin on the street or that it hits one like winning a lottery; rather, it is something that one constructs, brick by brick, like a house."[23]

## The Present and the Ordinary

To find the path of happiness, one has to consider time as well, not only in the sense that being happy takes time, but also with regard to the fact that real happiness has to be found in the *present time*, more than in the past or in the future. "I would like to cry out to my friends that the only way of being alive is to live in the present. That there is no way of being happy if one is not being happy today. That flights to the past or to the future are just that: flights. That a person who really

23. Jose Luis Martín Descalzo, *Razones para la alegría* (Madrid: Sociedad de Educación Atenas, 1998), 14.

wants to live should shout to himself in front of the mirror, each day as he gets up, that the day that is beginning is the most important of his life. The past has passed—it serves only for climbing onto it in order to see forward better. The future will come from the hands of God, and it has to be left in them. Our only task is the present; this hour is it."[24]

The danger consists, then, in not valuing the present reality and in fleeing from it, dedicating oneself to idealizing the past or awaiting everything from the future. People who do not risk their present with the light proper to happiness are constructing a tunnel in which happiness is found only at the beginning (in the past) and at the end (in the future). To be happy in the present, it is essential to identify with the present reality. Seneca states, "He is happy who in his present circumstances, whatever they may be, is satisfied and on friendly terms with the conditions of his life."[25] We might add that this is valid when those circumstances correspond

---

24. Descalzo, 76.

25. Seneca, *Minor Dialogues*, p. 211.

to our individual identities as humans and are in accord with our unique situations in life—for example, provided that they are consistent with the will of God—for if they are not, we have to make the changes necessary to attain that consistency.

Another subtle way of evading the present consists in letting ourselves be led by what we like and not by what we must do. Take, for example, the father who, instead of attending to his children, avoids them through social life or work, or the student who substitutes sports or other diversions for his books. If we abandon our obligations, "even the most ordinary things, which are licit and which bring a bit of happiness, would then become as bitter as gall, as sour as vinegar, and as repugnant as arum."[26]

There is also danger in thinking, as many do, that happiness is found in the extraordinary, in the spectacular, in those moments that we long for, precisely because these are exceptional, isolated, and passing:

26. Josemaría Escrivá, *Friends of God* (New York: Scepter, 2002), 183.

momentary successes, a particular adventure, a trip that we have wanted for a long time, a special weekend, or the end-of-year holidays. If deep happiness must be characterized by its permanence, either we find it in ordinary life or we never find it. Happy people are happy when they carry out the duties that habitually occupy their lives: work, family life,[27] their relationship with God, social relationships and friendships, study and formation, sports and other recreational activities.[28]

In this context, we have to conclude that the greater part of the multiple pieces that make up happiness is found precisely in the ordinary, and, to the extent that these pieces are added up, happiness is constructed. What increases our happiness is principally the events of daily life more than the extraordinary moments. Reciprocally, "trivial matters, in themselves foreign to happiness, are

---

27. "Asked, 'What is necessary for your happiness?' or 'What is it that makes your life meaningful?' most people, however, mention—before anything else—satisfying close relationships with family, friends, or romantic partners." David G. Myers, *The Pursuit of Happiness* (New York: Quill, 2002), p. 150.

28. Paul Poupard, Felicidad y fe cristiana (Barcelona: Herder, 1992),19.

transformed when one is happy. Most of our occupations—going through our chores, from morning to night—have little importance. . . . but, if we are happy, these occupations become transfigured and acquire a kind of halo."[29]

In summary, we could say that happiness is an interior task; it depends on choices that rest on our internal dispositions, on the orientation of our conduct and on our being; and it is carried out in the present and in ordinary life. Now let us ask ourselves: if attaining happiness is an interior task, is it enough to renounce seeking it outside of ourselves, or is it necessary also to sort out internal obstacles?

---

29. Marías, 248.

3

CHAPTER

# Resentment and Envy

## Obstacles to Happiness

As humans, we have a strong inclination to revolve around ourselves, to place "I" at the center of our thoughts and as the point of reference for our actions. This inclination, called *egocentrism*, is the antithesis of self-forgetfulness; it is the polar opposite of putting others first. Egocentrism generates sadness and discontent, which can ultimately provoke an interior collapse. If we live with excessive concern about ourselves, concentrating primarily on our own egos, we will likely lose objective vision and become hypersensitive and vulnerable. We will be affected by circumstances, suffering in a disproportionate way and incapable of enjoying the good that life offers us. "One of the things that makes man saddest is *ego latria* (self-worship), frequently the origin of useless sufferings, produced by an excessive preoccupation with the personal, overly exaggerating its importance."[1]

Egocentrism shows itself in various ways. Two of these constitute great obstacles to happiness and are worth considering in some detail in order to understand them, detect them in one's personal life, and resolve them as soon as possible. They are resentment and envy.

## The Poison of Resentment

Resentment is the principal obstacle to being happy[2] because it embitters the spirit. Max Scheler calls resentment a poisoning of our mind[3] that usually appears as a reaction to a negative stimulus in the form of an offense

---

1. Rojas, 235.

2. See Francisco Ugarte, *From Resentment to Forgiveness: A Gateway to Happiness* (New York: Scepter, 2012).

3. Max Scheler, *Ressentiment* (Wisconsin: Marquette University Press, 1994).

or an aggressive act. Obviously, not every offense produces resentment, but all resentment is preceded by an offense.

The offense that causes resentment can present itself as an action of "him against me, come by way of *omission*, or be attributed to circumstances such as one's socioeconomic situation, a physical defect, or an infirmity that engenders exclusion. In any case, the stimulus that provokes resentment can be judged with *objectivity* or with *exaggeration*, and it may even be entirely the product of *imagination*. The degree of resentment depends on how we judge the offenses against us, which explains the fact that many resentments are unwarranted, based on imagined or exaggerated situations or acts that have either not occurred or were not at all intentional.

## The Personal Response

Resentment is a negative reaction in the face of aggression, an adverse response to the offense. It is not the only option, as freedom gives humans the power to direct our reactions. Stephen Covey holds that "it is not what others do or even our own mistakes that hurt us the most; it is our response to thoses things. Chasing after the poisonous snake that bites us will only drive the poison through our entire system. It is far better to take measures immediately to get the poison out."[4] This alternative presents itself in the case of every aggression: either we concentrate on the one who has offended us (and the poison continues to act) or we eliminate it with an adequate response, not allowing it to remain within us.

The difficulty in giving the correct response is rooted in the fact that resentment is at the emotional level of the personality. In essence, it is a feeling, a passion, a movement experienced through the senses. If I am resentful, I feel myself injured or offended by someone or something that has attacked me as a person, and managing feelings is not an easy job. Sometimes we are not conscious of them—which means that emotions can be acting within us without our realizing

4. Stephen R. Covey, *The 7 Habits of Highly Effective People*, (New York: Free Press, 1994), p. 91.

it—whereas in other cases the resentment is reinforced by reasons that justify it, when we not only feel hurt but consider ourselves to have been legitimately offended.

## The Intervention of the Intelligence and the Will

These difficulties can be mitigated if we make good use of the ability to think. Self-knowledge and reflection allow us to connect the manifestations of our resentments with their causes and, to this extent, we find ourselves able to channel them. If, when analyzing the offense, we make an effort to understand the offender's way of acting and to discover factors that might explain it, then our negative reaction may disappear as the stimulus shrinks. Human intelligence thus can influence us indirectly. Aristotle spoke of a political though not despotic domination of the intellect over one's feelings; in order to avoid or eliminate resentments, we can modify the effects things and people have on us.

Another reliable resource is to cast out the wound without retaining it, including those from real offenses. "No one can make you feel inferior without your consent" Eleanor Roosevelt has been credited as saying. Similarly, Spanish doctor and thinker Gregorio Marañon noted, "Man reacts strongly with direct energy against aggression and automatically expels the aggression from his consciousness, like a foreign body. This saving elasticity does not exist in a resentful person."[5] If, in contrast, the will is weak, the offense is retained, and the feeling remains within the subject, who experiences it over and over again, even though considerable time may have passed. Resentment consists precisely of reliving the emotion, renewing the original feeling.[6]

The struggle against resentment will be much more effective if we count on the help of God, who clarifies our intelligence, favoring objectivity in our knowledge and capacity for understanding. God strengthens our will and fortifies our character so that it does not bow to the oppression of grievances.

---

5. Gregorio Marañon, *Tiberio: Historía de un resentimiento*, (Madrid: Espasa-Calpe, 1981), p. 29.

6. Scheler, *Ressentiment.*

## Feeling and Resentment

Our ways of reacting to a stimulus are usually closely related to individual temperament. For example, an emotional person *feels* an aggression more than a person who is not emotional; the former usually *retains* the reaction to an offensive stimulus longer than the latter. Those who are active in moderating their own emotional health will seek out more resources to defray the impacts received from offenses than will those who are non-active. In addition, culture and education, together with genetic factors, influence our ways of reacting and, therefore, the manner in which our resentment originates and is manifested.

One mode of reacting to offense is passivity, simply retreating or distancing ourselves from an aggressor and avoiding interaction. Mexicans tend to use the verb "*sentirse*" for this. Joaquin Peñalosa explains that "'feel' (*sentirse*) is a reflexive verb that we could conjugate all day, but it is not easy to find a proper philological definition for the simple reason that the verb expresses the Mexican soul more than the Spanish language. Having a feeling for (*estar sentido con*) someone is the same as being pained, sad, or upset by someone who has snubbed us, sometimes really but much more often, only apparently."[7]

In contrast, when we have a feeling of susceptibility that includes an eagerness for vindication, for vengeance, it is then a matter of *resentment*, properly speaking, in the full sense of the term. We who hold the resentment not only feel the offense that was inflicted on us, but also unite with it a feeling of hostility toward the person who caused the harm, a rancor that impels us toward revenge.

It has been said that "resentment is like taking poison and waiting for the other person to die."[8] It may be that the person toward whom the rancor is directed is unaware, while the resentful one is being eaten up from within. As poison has destructive effects on an organism, resentment produces frustration, sadness, and bitterness in the soul. Resentment is one of the worst enemies of happiness because it prevents us from focusing

7. Joaquin Peñalosa, *El mexicano y los 7 pecados capitales*, (Paulinas, Mexico, 1985), p. 70.

8. Witchel, Alex, "At Lunch with Malachy McCourt: How a Rogue Turns Himself into a Saint," *New York Times*, July 29, 1998.

positively on life and distances us from God and from others.

Egocentric people have a special propensity for resentment; they overreact to stimuli of little importance, or they accumulate unfounded resentments. The origin of this inclination is usually found in *egocentrism*. Because egocentric people center all thoughts and actions on themselves, they become perpetually vulnerable and subject to chronic unhappiness. "Only if a person forgets himself and gives himself to God and to others . . . can he be happy on this earth, with a happiness that is a preparation for, and a foretaste of, the joy of heaven."[9] Self-forgetfulness is the best antidote against resentment, because it strongly reduces the subjective resonance of injuries and the likelihood of keeping them alive.

## The Remedy of Forgiveness

In the Old Testament the law of talion prevailed, inspired by strict justice: "eye for eye,

9. Escrivá, *Christ Is Passing By*, 24.

tooth for tooth." In coming to perfect the law, Jesus Christ introduced a fundamental modification, connecting justice with mercy, and further, subordinating justice to love, which was revolutionary. By Christ's teaching, offenses received must be forgiven, as forgiveness becomes an essential part of love.

The mercy that Jesus practiced and demanded from his followers collided not only with the feelings of his contemporaries but also with those from all times. "You have heard that it was said, 'You shall love your neighbor and hate your enemy.' But I say to you, Love your enemies and pray for those who persecute you."[10] "To him who strikes you on the cheek, offer the other also; and from him who takes away your cloak do not withhold your coat as well."[11] These demands of love surpass the capacity of human nature. That is why Jesus invites his followers to a goal which has no limits; only from there are they able to attempt what he asks of them: "Be merciful, even as your Father is merciful."[12]

10. Mt 5:43–44.

11. Lk 6:29.

12. Lk 6:36.

## What Is Forgiveness?

In contrast to resentment, forgiving is an act, not a feeling. Forgiving does not mean one stops feeling. There are some who consider themselves incapable of forgiving certain grievances because they cannot eliminate their effects; they cannot stop experiencing the wound, nor the hatred, nor the desire for revenge. Here is where complications often arise with regard to moral conscience, especially if one takes into account that God forgives to the extent that we forgive. The incapacity to stop feeling the resentment can, in fact, be insuperable, at least in the short run. Nevertheless, if we understand that forgiveness is on a different level from resentment—that is, on the level of the will, we are then able to discover the path pointing to the solution.

Forgiveness is an act of the will because it consists in making a decision. In forgiving, I choose to cancel the moral debt that the other has contracted with me in offending me and, therefore, I free that person as a debtor. It is not suppressing the offense committed and causing it never to have existed, because we lack that power. Only God can erase the offensive act and return the offender to the state in which he existed before committing it. But we, when we truly forgive, desire that the other person be fully freed from the bad action that he committed. As Leonardo Polo points out, "To forgive implies asking God to forgive, because only in that way is the offense annihilated."[13]

## Forgive and Forget

If the act of forgiving consists in making a decision, the act of forgetting, in contrast, does not. Forgetting takes place in the memory, which does not respond directly to commands of the will. I can decide to forget an offense, but I may not succeed. The offense may remain in the archive of my memory, despite my command. In this way, forgetting is not the same as forgiving. An eloquent sign that we have forgiven, albeit without forgetting, is that the recollection of the offense

13. Leonardo Polo, *Quién es el hombre* (Madrid: Rialp, 1998), p. 140.

has no effect on how we act with those we have forgiven; we deal with them as though we have forgotten the offense altogether. True forgiveness demands that we operate in this way, because true love does not brood over injury.[14]

On the other hand, the expression "I forgive, but I will not forget" means that, basically, I do not want to forget the offense, which is the equivalent of not wanting to forgive. Why? When I forgive, I cancel the debt of the offender, which is incompatible with the intention of retaining it, of not wanting to forget it. Consequently, although we cannot identify forgiveness with the act of forgetting the offense, we can say that *to forgive is to want to forget.*

## Why Forgive?

When we forgive, we free ourselves from the slavery produced by hatred and resentment and can then recover the happiness once blocked by those sentiments. It also makes

14. See 1 Cor 13:5.

a lot of sense to forgive with regard to interacting with others. If we do not forgive, love is chilled or even turned into hatred, and friendship can be lost forever.

In addition to human motives for forgiving, there are supernatural reasons that make it possible to forgive in extreme situations where human arguments are not enough. God gave us free will and with it, we are capable of loving him or of offending him by sin. If we choose to offend him, he offers forgiveness if we repent, but he has established a condition for that, which is that we must first forgive the neighbor who has injured us. This is what we express in the prayer that Jesus taught us, "Forgive us our trespasses, as we forgive those who trespass against us." We have to ask ourselves why God conditions his divine forgiveness on our human forgiveness and, even more, demands that we forgive our enemies unconditionally, even those who do not want to make amends. God is not trying to make our paths difficult; he always wants the best for us. He deeply wants to forgive us, but his forgiveness will not penetrate us if our inner dispositions are unchanged. "In refusing to forgive our brothers and sisters, our hearts are closed, and their hardness makes them impervious to the Father's merciful love."[15]

Besides that occasion on which he taught the Our Father, Jesus insisted many other times on the need for forgiving. When Peter asked if he ought to forgive as many as seven times, the answer was to forgive *seventy times seven*,[16] because forgiveness has no limits; Christ asked us to forgive even our enemies, to do them good in return for evil.[17] For the Christian, these teachings constitute a powerful case for forgiveness, for they were dictated by the Master.

Jesus, who is the model to follow, not only preached forgiveness but also practiced it innumerable times. In his life, we find abundant deeds that demonstrate his capacity for forgiveness, which is likely what best showed the love in his heart. While the scribes and Pharisees accused a woman taken in adultery, Jesus forgave her and told her not

---

15. *Catechism of the Catholic Church*, 2840.

16. See Mt 18:21–22.

17. See Mt 5:44.

to sin again;[18] when they brought a paralytic on a pallet for him to cure, Jesus first forgave the man's sins;[19] when Peter denied him three times, in spite of his warning, Jesus looked at him to elicit a reaction [20] and then not only forgave him but also restored his full confidence, leaving him at the head of his Church. The climax of Jesus' forgiveness took place on the Cross, when he prayed for those who were killing him: "Father, forgive them; for they know not what they do."[21]

The consideration that sin is an offense against God, that the offense acquires infinite dimensions because it is God who is offended, and that in spite of that, God forgives our sins when we do our part, permits us to see the disproportion that exists between divine forgiveness and human forgiveness. Therefore, even those offenses that seem unforgivable—because of their magnitude, because they are against innocent persons, or because of the consequences stemming from them—must

18. See Jn 8:3–11.

19. See Mk 2:5.

20. See Lk 22:56–61.

21. Lk 23:34.

be forgiven because "there is no limit or measure to this essentially divine forgiveness."[22] Hence, in order to forgive radically, one needs the help of God.

Forgiving is the highest expression of love and, consequently, is what transforms the human heart the most. Therefore, each time that we forgive, an interior conversion is worked in us, a true metamorphosis to the degree that made St. John Chrysostom exclaim, "Nothing makes us more similar to God than being ready to forgive,"[23] from which one can conclude that forgiving is the principal remedy for resentment.

## The Problem of Envy

As with resentment, envy "is a serious obstacle to happiness"[24] and includes the aggravating circumstance that it is difficult to recognize in ourselves. We seldom hear others

---

22. *CCC*, 2845.

23. John Chrysostom as quoted in Dmitri Royster, *The Kingdom of God: The Sermon on the Mount* (Crestwood, NY: St. Vladimir's Seminary Press, 1992), p. 86.

24. Rojas, p. 323.

say they are envious, even if they don't find it a problem to admit they are ambitious, disorderly, proud, or intemperate. In a competitive world like ours, the tendency toward envy has become acute. Thomas Aquinas defines envy as becoming saddened by the good of another—and viewing that good as a factor that decreases one's own excellence or happiness.[25] Let's take a look at each of these ideas.

## The Sadness of Envy

Sadness appears as an immediate and direct effect of envy. If joy is derived from the possession of a good, sadness is caused by our relationship to an evil. When we lose a beloved person, fail in a professional project, or suffer a grave illness, we feel saddened by the adverse events. To experience sadness in these cases is natural; the lack of that good can be seen as an evil. However, there exists the possibility of overcoming it and, without ceasing to feel the sorrow that it brings, finding meaning in the experience.

---

25. See Aquinas, *Summa Theologica* 2–2.36.2.

In contrast, envy consists in being saddened by someone else's *good.* In that case, we find ourselves facing a different and rather surprising situation: the cause of our sadness is not an evil but a *good.* This is not natural, because a *good* usually produces *joy.* If the outcome, instead, is sadness, we experience difficulty in justifying the reaction. Moreover, the abnormality of such a response to a good makes that response shameful, and we instinctively try to hide it. This explains the difficulty of our recognizing envy in ourselves; it is not easy to justify sadness in the face of something good. Hence we try to disguise it, although not always with success. Children, who lack duplicity, cannot hide this; they tend to display it with all naturalness. We have all seen the violent reaction of one child snatching a toy from another or the tears of a young child at the sight of a sibling receiving a gift.

Why does the good of another cause us sadness? The answer is not in the good itself, but in our ways of perceiving or judging it. We perceive the good as something that we are lacking, a reality that, fundamentally, we do not accept. The non-acceptance of our lack leads us to look at our neighbor's good in a twisted way, which translates into disharmony with the one who possesses it. If we accept our limitations with peace and are content with who we are and what we have, we are not upset by the good of others; in fact, we can feel happy. And in this case, rejoicing in the merits of others is acting in conformity with the will of God.[26]

Therefore, envy is rooted in egocentrism, which takes the form of *comparison*. Our own selves become the point of reference for the values that we discover in others; instead of looking at them objectively, as qualities worthy of admiration, we view them in a negative way, as something that we lack. This deviation in focus produces sadness by its egocentric effect because it concentrates attention on the negative: our lack of those values. If we were capable of discovering the good that

---

26. "But it is not this, he will say, that grieves me, for I should wish God to be glorified by me. Well then! rejoice at thy brother's being in honor, and then glorified is God again through thee also; and all will say, Blessed be God that hath His household so minded, wholly freed from envy, and rejoicing together at one another's goods!" St. John Chrysostom, *Homilies on Romans* 7.31.

exists in others—*without comparing ourselves* to them and with a generous disposition, truly open to the good of our neighbors—there would be no envy.

## A Defect in Outlook

Envy, as we have seen, arises from a defect in our *way of looking at* the good of others. The Latin derivation of the word refers to a mistaken way of looking at something; it comes from the Latin word *invidia*, which means "to see with bad eyes," with a twisted look that negatively interprets what is positive: the good. This twisted view can also create a problem in considering the good itself. Seneca observed that those who spend too much time focusing on the possessions of others fail to appreciate their own things. In contrast, we who know how to be satisfied with what we have, or, even better, to be thankful for it, can enjoy it without being disturbed by the good things of others.

If we take another step and ask ourselves why the envious person feels negatively affected by discovering the good of someone else, we can find the answer in the last part of the afore-mentioned affirmations of St. Thomas Aquinas: it is because one sees that good as a factor which *diminishes* one's own excellence or happiness. Consider me, for example, comparing myself with others and in some way reckoning my own personal value as coming out ahead in those comparisons. If I value myself because I am better than the other, because I have more possessions than he does or because I surpass him in one aspect or another, then I cease to value myself insofar as I see myself surpassed. Every positive element that arises in the other diminishes me and, in consequence, I am saddened by it.

## Manifestations of Envy

It takes a lot to recognize ourselves as envious, but even if we try to hide it, there are some indicators that reveal our envy to a keen observer. All manifestations of envy seek to reduce in some way the good of another in order to compensate for the bad effect it has provoked in us. Perhaps the most evident is *negative criticism*, which tries to emphasize deficiencies that subtract value from the one envied. There is also defamation, which consists in propagating negative facts that harm the reputation of the other person. In a more subtle way, there can be *silence* or *apparent indifference* before the merits of the others, which might reveal an envy we attempt to hide. There may also be a kind of *resistance* or *block* that prevents us from seeing objectively and with a positive outlook what others do—their successes, their personal values; this could also be a subtle manifestation of envy. Resorting to *joking* or using *irony* regarding the qualities or successes of others frequently aims to reduce their importance because of the envy they produce in us. The envious person finds it hard to praise. When compelled to do so, faced with factual evidence, the person feels obliged to add something that reduces the praise: "*So and so is very intelligent, but not very refined; someone else has a lot of professional prestige, but is egoistical,*" and so on. In the best of cases, we have to recognize that the person in question is a good architect or a competent doctor if there is no way to get around it.

Envy can also have bodily manifestations. Because the human being forms a unit, the physical can affect the mind—such as the state of health having repercussions on the state of the soul. Just as shame reddens the face, envy seems to reduce the circulation of blood, which creates a pale face. Hence, in some countries, people speak of "pale" envy or, more often, of "livid" envy. The Spanish proverb by poet Francisco de Quevedo said, "Envy is so thin and pale because it bites but doesn't eat."

Finally, there is a peculiar version of envy that manifests with great evidence its malice and consists in *rejoicing in evil that afflicts another.* It entails a leisurely enjoyment of each misfortune that befalls another person.

## The Inclination to Envy

Although anyone can feel envy, some have a special propensity to it. Thomas Aquinas said those who tend to be envious include those ambitious for honors, the pusillanimous, and the aged.[27] Setting aside the last group, whose

27. See Aquinas, *Summa Theologica* 2–2.36.1.3 and 4.

inclination to envy might originate in difficulty accepting the limitations imposed by age, let us look at the other two cases. The *pusillanimous*, those lacking in courage, usually suffer from a feeling of inferiority that leads to feeling aggrieved by anything that seems superior to them and causes them to consider themselves diminished. That sentiment seems linked to the insecurity provoked by various factors, some of which might include failures that have not been internally resolved, lack of results in the fulfillment of their obligations or proposed goals, and physical defects that they have not accepted.

The solution here is, on the one hand, to accept their own limitations and, on the other hand, to become conscious of their own personal value and capacities, which are usually greater than they admit or realize. Doing so would allow them to make the best use of their abilities, with regard to both personal development and service of others.

Those who are *ambitious for honor* are especially exposed to envy by their egocentrism and vanity. They possess a disordered eagerness to be outstanding in everything, and they cannot stand to see themselves surpassed by anyone. When this occurs, they feel that an exclusive right has been usurped, and envy does not delay in making an appearance. The effect is sadness, which can turn into frustration or even into resentment, accompanied by a violent, vengeful reaction.

## The Nature of Envy

In accord with the structure and constitution of the human person, we have to distinguish the various dimensions of envy. In the first place, envy is a feeling, a passion, as Garcia Hoz notes: "In the psychological panorama, envy occupies a place among the higher feelings. . . . It is a reaction against that which, by its mere fact of being superior, affects us disagreeably. What is fundamental is the consciousness of one's own inferiority."[28] As a passion, envy may bypass a person's rational level, resulting in loss of self-control and leading to violent and uncontrolled reactions, such as may be seen in various passages of

28. Victor Garcia Hoz, *Pedagogía de la lucha ascética* (Madrid: Rialp, 1963), p. 248.

Sacred Scripture. Because of envy, Cain murdered his brother Abel,[29] Esau hated Jacob,[30] Joseph's brothers sold him into slavery,[31] Saul tried to kill David,[32] and Jesus was condemned to death.[33]

Envy is also an *act of the will*, endowed—because it is voluntary—with freedom. Because it goes against the order established by God, "envy is a capital sin. It refers to the sadness at the sight of another's goods and the immoderate desire to acquire them for oneself, even unjustly."[34] From the moral point of view, we have to differentiate between a free act of the will and the mere feeling of an emotional tendency. Regarding this last, if I do not *consent*, if my will rejects the bad inclination and tries to counteract it,[35] then it is not a sin. Finally,

29. See Gn 4:3–8.

30. See Gn 27:41.

31. See Gn 37:4–28.

32. See 1 Sm 16—19.

33. See Mk 15:10; Mt 27:18.

34. *CCC*, 2539.

35. "If you cut any hint of envy out at the roots, and if you sincerely rejoice in other people's success, you will not lose your cheerfulness." Josemaría Escrivá, *Furrow* in *The Way, Furrow, The Forge* (New York: Scepter, 2001), 93.

when free acts are repeated on successive occasions, they usually give rise to habits that, if they are bad, are called *vices*. Thus envy becomes a vice if the act is repeated again and again. When the vice is joined by passion, the consequences can be unforeseeable. "Envy is at the same time a vice and a passion; the first is opposed to virtue and the second falls on the plane of the affections, but as something that is so overwhelming, that has such power through its content, that being something emotional is capable of overstepping the intellectual level and provoking in it a blindness of its faculties."[36] Therefore envy not only goes against the happiness of the envious person who suffers from it but also, in some cases, against the one envied.

*Emulation* is the other face of envy and, in a sense, its positive side. To emulate is to imitate, with healthy competitiveness, the triumphs and positive examples observed in other people. This does not work against happiness. Therefore, in colloquial language we can speak of healthy envy or good envy;

---

36. Rojas, 311.

we can bring ourselves, thanks to an effort of the will—stimulated by another's triumph—to high human enterprises. In the supernatural order, we can also speak of *holy envy*.[37]

## Solutions to Envy

We can see clearly the gravity of envy. Schopenhauer believed there was nothing more implacable and cruel than envy.[38] As for the serious obstacle that it implies for happiness, what means can help to overcome it? We find the solution in all that favors the capacity to "rejoice over the goods of others," which is precisely the contrary of envy. The adequate dispositions for this include the following:

1) *Accepting ourselves,* including our defects and strengths, in order to allow us to accept others, with their values and accomplishments.

37. "You might have thought occasionally, with holy envy, about the adolescent Apostle John, *quem diligebat Iesus*—whom Jesus loved. Wouldn't you like to deserve to be called 'the one who loves the Will of God?' Then take the necessary steps, day after day." Escrivá, *The Forge*, 422.

38. Arthur Schopenhauer, *The Basis of Morality*, 2nd ed., trans. A.B. Bullock (New York: Dover Publications, Inc., 2005), p. 78.

2) *Choosing not to compare ourselves egocentrically with others*—nor make judgments about ourselves based on such comparisons. We must apply comparisons positively instead, with the intention of improving (*emulation*).

3) *Cultivating self-forgetfulness and service of our neighbors,* in order to grow in humility and develop high esteem for those around us.

4) *Fostering magnanimity, forgiving ourselves with greatness of spirit,* to eradicate all feelings of inferiority.

5) *Loving others* so that we see their progress, their qualities, and their successes as contributors to our own joy.

6) *Recognizing ourselves as loved by God,* taking into account that the human person is "the only creature on earth which God willed for himself."[39]

39. Paul VI, *Gaudium et spes*, Pastoral Constitution on the Church in the Modern World, December 7, 1965, 24.3, Vatican website: *http://www.vatican.va/archive/hist_councils/ii_vatican_council/documents/vat-ii_const_19651207_gaudium-et-spes_en.html.*

4

CHAPTER

# Optimism Leads to Happiness

## What Studies Reveal

Optimism has many benefits. For example, it influences physical health, as indicated by the following data: Researchers evaluated 122 men who had experienced a first heart attack to determine their degrees of optimism or pessimism. "Eight years later, of the 25 most pessimistic men, 21 had died; of the 25 most optimistic, just 6 had died. Their mental outlook proved a better predictor of survival than any medical risk factor, including the amount of damage to the heart in the first attack, artery blockage, cholesterol level, or blood pressure.[1] These results obviously justify an interest in optimism, given that health is a relevant value in human life, but there is a more weighty reason to consider its importance more deeply, and that is its close relationship to happiness.

An American research study set out to check a hundred *happy people*, to determine if there was any common denominator that might prove the key to uncovering the source or essence of happiness. The method of selecting the people consisted in carrying out interviews and seeking a triple coincidence that would allow a determination that they really were happy. These were as follows: the person interviewed felt and declared him or herself very happy; the person appeared to his family and closest friends to be very happy; and the researchers who did the interviewing also perceived this. Once the selection was made, the researchers noted that more than half of those hundred people—exactly 70 percent—came from small towns or cities, but this could not provide the key they were

1. Daniel Goleman, *Emotional Intelligence* (New York: Bantam, 1997), p. 177.

seeking. Finally, the researchers found themselves forced to coin a new word to describe what they found in those happy people: all of them were "good-finders;" they had the capacity to find the good in everything and in everyone,[2] which coincides to a great degree, as we shall see, with optimism.

In the results of the aforementioned study on happiness by David G. Myers and Ed Diener, one of the four characteristic features of happy people is optimism.[3] The researchers did not conclude whether the optimism is a cause of the happiness or if the person is optimistic because he or she is happy. They simply noted the fact that those who are happy are optimistic. But this is sufficient to realize the intimate relationship that optimism has with happiness.

## Naïve, Misguided, or Enthusiastic "Optimism"

In common language, when we say that someone is highly optimistic, we might envision

2. See Poupard, pp. 23–24, and Powell, p. 114.

3. The other three features that they discovered were a high degree of self-esteem, control over their own lives, and, in the majority of cases, being extroverted. See Myers and Diener.

a person who is naïve or unrealistic, not seeing the objective problems or difficulties but viewing everything superficially and only in its "positive" dimension. The person seems to have failed to contemplate things as they are and to reflect about them objectively. But optimism certainly doesn't coincide with this naïve attitude, which is disconnected from reality. When people who profess *naïve optimism* face a circumstance that opens their eyes to harsh realities, they suffer deep confusion and may fall to pieces. That is not the case for a true optimist. True optimism is based on reality—the truth—for only thus does it acquire consistency. Nor does optimism coincide with an illusory attitude, characteristic of someone who lives on illusions, lacking foundation and hoping that the future in its entirety will be favorable and will unfold without difficulty. In those cases, what is lacking is a deeper knowledge of present reality and future expectations, as well as an objective evaluation of known reality and of what is to come. Having an illusionary attitude is not the same as having dreams and hopes in life, which are factors that strongly favor optimism and happiness.

It could also be that if we say someone is highly optimistic, we might imagine an enthusiastic or even euphoric temperament that reacts in an exaggerated way to ordinary stimuli, one which attributes a disproportionate value to facts that merit a more modest valuation. In this case, it is important to note that optimism is not identified with a simple state of mind, with no greater foundation than one's own temperament. How often do we find that those "enthusiasts," of whom we expect valiant actions, fear to make decisions that include risks or easily become discouraged in the face of obstacles? This does not mean that the spontaneously enthusiastic temperament is a negative; on the contrary, it can be an important aid in life, but it is necessary that it be developed for balance and consistency. "The optimistic temperament is something appealing and useful in the face of the anxieties of life: who does not rejoice in the face of the joy and confidence that radiates from a person? Who doesn't wish this for himself? Like all natural dispositions, an optimism of this kind is above all a morally neutral quality; like all dispositions it should be developed and cultivated in order to positively form the moral make-up of a person. However, it can grow through Christian hope and become something more pure and profound; on the contrary, in an empty and false existence it can decay and become a pure façade."[4]

If one's optimism does not depend solely on temperament, it is because one was not "determined" from the beginning to be either optimistic or pessimistic. In some cases, the temperament might be inclined toward optimism—to see and interpret facts positively—and in others toward pessimism—to see the negative before the positive. Nevertheless, in this second case, the inclinations can be overcome by firm decisions of the will—by personal choices—that influence our ways of perceiving and evaluating reality, as well as in our interior attitudes. "We observe that with the same grape one can obtain wine and vinegar. We have to make a decision. In our heart there isn't room for two presses, two types of fermentation: we either choose the vinegar of bitterness or we prefer the wine of joy. Each of us is called upon to make his own personal

4. Joseph Ratzinger, *Mirar a Cristo* (Valencia: edicep, 1990), p. 51.

choice."[5] In other words, the determinant is not in the facts—the grape is the same—but in the ways of looking at it and the attitudes with which we confront them. Ordinarily we are not able to change the facts, but we can direct our perceptions and attitudes. We can look at the grape either as that which will eventually yield wine and rejoice in that possibility, or see it only as the prime matter for vinegar. The decision is in our hands, as is reflected in the old rhyme: *Two men looked out from prison bars. One saw mud, the other stars.* If I choose optimism and keep my choices consistent throughout my path, it becomes a stable quality of my personality, a way of being. On the contrary, I could give in to pessimism, a dangerous sickness that it is well worth the effort to avoid.

## The Threat of Pessimism

On the other extreme from naïve, misguided, or simply enthusiastic optimism is pessimism, which means accentuating the negative aspects of reality. Pessimism is that disposition

5. Rafael Llano, *Optimismo* (Mexico City: MiNos, 1994), 23.

of seeing the glass half empty, instead of half full, of capturing the darkness instead of the light, the thorns instead of the roses, the problems instead of the solutions, and the defects without appreciating the positive qualities. In forgetting the positive, the pessimist finds nourishment in negative elements, both real and imaginary, and ends up not being objective.

We frequently run into people inclined to pessimism. Some are pessimistic simply by temperament; for example, a person who is *reactive* has greater difficulties in adapting to complex situations and will easily renounce them. Others adopt a dark view owing to *family influence*; a child whose mother is pessimistic will ordinarily be so, too, having been exposed to a steady stream of negative explanations and focuses from an early age. Parents may be pessimistic because their defects weigh on them more than their positive qualities and, in consequence, they have low *self-esteem*.[6] Or perhaps they retain

6. "Our feelings towards ourselves, the way we evaluate our efficacy, or our capacity to carry out tasks or confront problems, is not just one more feeling, but can contribute as an ingredient to many feelings." José Antonio Marina, 157.

*negative experiences* of their own lives, having not learned how to overcome the effects of their mistakes or failures, much less to see them as opportunities for growth or learning. To these causes of pessimism one could add others that are more profound, in particular *agnosticism*, which deprives human beings of the possibility of finding support for life in God and of finding in him the true response to life's difficulties.

## Means of Overcoming Pessimism

Here I'll point out some means for overcoming pessimism that I'll expand upon later when discussing the keys of optimism.

1) *Turn your attention from the negative.* The pessimist feels habitually inclined toward negative thoughts and experiences, both in the present and in the future, in the real and in the imaginary. It was what Don Quixote recommended to the page: "And bear in mind what I am now about to say to you for it will be of great use and comfort to you in time of trouble; it is, not to let your mind dwell on the

adverse chances that may befall you."[7] If we possess or acquire the ability to resist thinking negatively in the midst of adverse events, we will have an effective resource for protecting our happiness. Speaking in affirmative terms, we should discover and concentrate on the positive. As a practical exercise, we might each write a list of the favorable things that have arisen in our personal lives and surroundings, as well as of the possibilities life may offer in the future.

2) *Learn to clarify and minimize errors,* taking away their absolute character (which the pessimist subjectively attributes to them: "Since I failed in this, I am of no use; since I was mistaken in that other thing, I am definitely disqualified"). In short, it's a matter of evaluating negative events with objectivity, not giving them an importance that they don't have, and reducing their emotional impact so that they don't take on more importance than they deserve. The example below illustrates this. A man who had lost all of his money

7. de Cervantes, Miguel, *Complete Works of Miguel de Cervantes*, trans. John Ormsby (UK: Delphi Classics, 2013), digital version.

made a phone call to a friend who had a lot of common sense. The conversation went as follows:

"I'm finished; I've lost everything, I don't have anything left."

"Can you still see?" his friend asked.

"Yes, I can still see."

"Can you still walk?" his friend asked next.

"Yes, I can still walk."

"It's obvious that you can still speak and hear, otherwise we wouldn't be communicating."

"You're right on that, too."

"Then it's obvious that you still have everything," his friend concluded. "The only thing you've lost is your money!"

3) *Avoid complaints and lamentations,* both external and internal, which are usually sterile because they only succeed in generating a victim mentality, with a strong egocentric burden that invites one to passivity and, in the best of cases, to resignation. Avoiding complaints may require great effort in some circumstances, or for some personalities, because it implies overcoming a negative reality, or one that we think is negative, in order to find a solution. Those who have faith in God

can count on a perspective which permits us more easily and deeply to see the meaning in adverse situations, especially those which are humanly inexplicable, such as an incurable sickness or the death of a loved one who is still young. "Don't be a pessimist. Don't you realize that all that happens or can happen is for the best? Your optimism will be a necessary consequence of your faith."[8]

## The Nature of Optimism

I have pointed out that there are people who are spontaneously optimistic, which means that they have optimistic temperaments. In these cases, the emotional factor usually plays an important role insofar as it implies an impulse to perceive reality positively, without any express effort of the will. The intellect simply finds itself inclined in that direction, accompanied by emotion or enthusiasm. At this level, one can also speak of a temperamental or emotional optimism—of a *feeling*—very valuable when it arises, but limited because of

---

8. Josemaría Escrivá, *The Way* (New York: Scepter, 2002), 378.

its eventual instability. It is well known that if our feelings do not have the support of our wills, they lack stability and can reverse themselves at any moment.

I have mentioned that being optimistic depends on a personal choice, that is, on a decision rooted in the will. The will can influence the intellect, ordaining it to perceive reality in a positive way, which seeks and finds goodness in the makeup of things. In this case, we can say that optimism is an *attitude*; the will disposes the intellect so that it perceives the good and values it in such a way that those perceptions influence the whole person—including and with special importance on emotions. This approach results in a favorable and vital tone that, in turn, influences the will and the intellect, reinforcing the person's disposition to perceive the good. This virtuous circle inclines us to think that authentic optimism includes the whole being: the intellect as well as the will and the emotions.

It is also worthwhile to note that if we maintain a consistent attitude of optimism in various situations, we turn it into a habit, which constitutes a *permanent* disposition of perceiving and valuing the present and potential good in everything around us, beginning with ourselves. Since it is a matter of a good habit, one can say, with all rigor, that optimism is a *virtue.*

It is encouraging that optimism, whose influence on happiness is crucial, depends in good measure on a personal choice. This justifies us in going further and asking what *keys of optimism* allow us to cultivate it and develop it in our own lives so that happiness grows to that same degree.

## Keys to Optimism

### 1) *Discover and value the positive*

Most people have to make a concerted effort to detect the goodness that exists in the reality of their lives: not only is evil present in one form or another, but, also, we easily grow accustomed even to the best things and thus overlook them, failing to appreciate them. To be optimistic is precisely to escape from mediocrity, "to discover and enjoy all the good that we have. Not to have to wait to meet a blind person to realize the beauty and importance of having sight. And not having to meet a deaf person to discover the wonder of hearing. To get joy from the fact that our hands can move without having to make this discovery by seeing the 'dead hands' of a paralytic."[9] According to St. Thomas Aquinas, it involves focusing our attention more on the good than on the bad.[10]

This capacity of discovering the positive nourishes the spirit with good things, while at the same time generating sentiments that lead to optimism and happiness. An optimistic person usually detects positive aspects in the same proportion that a pessimist discovers negative ones, as one researcher demonstrated: in their respective interpretations of a particular event, out of ten aspects, an unhappy person saw eight negatives, while a happy person—an optimist—saw eight positive aspects.[11] However, merely seeing the goodness of things could be compatible with

9. Descalzo, pp. 14–15.

10. Aquinas, *Summa Theologica* 2–2.106.3.2.

11. See Niven, p. 30.

a superficial outlook, which has little influence on our lives and our conduct. The *evaluation of the good* that we discover is an act distinct from simple discovery; it implies recognizing and deeply appreciating that which we have encountered in such a way that it influences the will and animates it to reinforce the positive attitude. Alphonse Kerr is one of several authors credited with expressing this observation: "Some people are always grumbling because roses have thorns. I am grateful because thorns have roses."

### 2) *Make positive suggestions*

Ordinarily, our ways of speaking follow our ways of thinking. Those who have superficial thoughts usually speak in a light way; those with complex ideas tend to be complicated in the ways they express themselves; those who continually criticize others condition their interior judgments toward bitterness. But it also happens that the manner of expressing ourselves can influence our ways of thinking. If I promise myself to speak only of positive things—silencing the negatives, which perhaps pass through my mind much more frequently—then over time, my thoughts and judgments will incline more and more toward the positive parts of reality rather than the negative. This change will make my future expressions more constructive, without my prompting, because they will manifest that new way of thinking optimistically.

3) *Possess self-esteem*

Self-esteem, correctly understood, depends on evaluating ourselves objectively, which includes recognizing and accepting both our good qualities and our defects, our potentialities as well as our limitations. This must always be approached with the confidence that those good qualities and possibilities, if used and enhanced, will ultimately be more important than defects and limitations as we develop our conduct. This focus is compatible with the virtue of humility, if one remembers that humility is knowing the truth about one's self. This objective and positive outlook forms an essential part of optimism and contributes considerably to happiness.

On the other hand, "one who is continually criticized easily develops a low level of self-esteem and needs to experience his own value in order to recognize his true potential, which the Biblical mandate of 'loving one's neighbor as oneself' establishes as the measure of love for others, the love one has for oneself."[12] Well-oriented self-esteem includes recognition and enjoyment of our accomplishments, without hiding our limitations. Crucial to this view is maintaining our humility (the truth) by attributing to God—who created us and maintains us in existence—all the good that we discover in our lives.

### 4) *Foster hope*

Optimism is intimately linked to hope as both a human and supernatural virtue. In general, hope consists in trusting in the means to attain the end that we have proposed to ourselves. Its influence in the attainment of objectives should be noted. "Hope, modern researchers are finding, does more than offer a bit of solace amid affliction; it plays a surprisingly potent role in life, offering an advantage in realms as diverse as school achievement

12. Poupard, p. 25.

and bearing up in onerous jobs. Hope, in a technical sense, is more than the sunny view that everything will turn out all right. Snyder defines it with more specificity as 'believing you have both the will and the way to accomplish your goals, whatever they may be.'"[13]

Hope, as is the case with optimism, can be learned and developed. When we acquire or perfect any kind of ability, we become more competent and increase confidence in our ability to meet challenges in other areas of life. If we meet these new challenges, our hope grows and, as a result, we become more optimistic. But humans are also called also to higher goals of a supernatural character, such as holiness, which logically exceed our purely human capacities. For that we need to have recourse to God, imploring his help. Here is precisely where hope as a supernatural virtue comes into play, in "the confident expectation of divine blessing."[14] As Cardinal Ratzinger noted, "A man without hope does not pray, because he does not hope; a man sure of his

13. Goleman, p. 87.

14. *CCC*, 2090.

ability and of himself does not pray because he trusts entirely in himself. One who prays hopes in a goodness and in a power that go beyond his own possibilities."[15] One who has hope, we can add, counts on a deep foundation for being optimistic because he has the sureness, both human and supernatural, of attaining what he wants.

### 5) *Take advantage of the results*

When we propose to carry out an ambitious project, we may adopt one of these attitudes to measure our advances: to concentrate on what we need to attain or to evaluate what we have already attained. The first weighs negatively on the spirit, while the second ordinarily produces optimism, which translates into an impetus to forge ahead. The same occurs with attainments in any other field of life; if we discover ourselves, recognize ourselves, and value ourselves, this produces self-confidence, and consequently, favors optimism and makes it grow. This attitude, as we have seen earlier, is compatible with recognizing our own defects and limitations, even

---

15. Ratzinger, *Mirar a Cristo*, p. 71.

while we must remain conscious that the ultimate origin of good results is in God rather than ourselves.

### 6) *Know how to win*

It's not hard to find people who *don't know how to win*, who are *losers*, because of their mental attitudes of insecurity and pessimism. If we, on the contrary, confront challenges with the confidence that we are going to win—that is, with "confidence of victory"—we considerably increase the probability that we will succeed. The boxer who climbs into the ring thinking he will lose the match usually loses it. In contrast, "the expectation of victory is already half the victory, because that optimistic disposition stimulates and opens broader points of view, apt to capture all of the resources that lead to success. In addition, it incites our energy, acts as a catalyst for the capacity that gives us a basic push, offers resistance and vitality to our spirit of struggle, and thus ends up creating conditions favorable to the good result of the project."[16]

16. R. Llano, pp. 18–19.

A consequence of possessing the attitude that trusts in victory is achieving the consistency needed to pursue goals when difficulties arise along the path. Here lies the evidence that optimism does not consist in a momentary enthusiasm, intense in the beginning but insufficient when the first obstacles arise. Various professional activities, such as selling insurance, quickly define whether candidates are optimistic or pessimistic by the ways they react to the high proportion of negative responses received from potential clients. Statistics reveal that about three quarters of these salespeople abandon the activity in the first three years. A MetLife study of insurance salespeople showed that optimistic new sellers sold 37% more insurance in their first two years than those who were pessimistic. The pessimists were also twice as likely to abandon their work during the first year.[17] Another consequence of a winning attitude is knowing how to take advantage of circumstances. A well-known quote, often credited to Churchill says, "An optimist sees

17. See Goleman, p. 89.

an opportunity in every calamity; a pessimist sees a calamity in every opportunity."

7) *Know how to lose*

What I've written above does not mean that we will always win our battles. It is necessary to mention that despite the right mental attitude and making use of the means, defeats will come. But it is necessary to adopt an optimistic attitude here, too, one consistent with *knowing how to lose*, which has several aspects:

a) Defeats help us to *know* ourselves better, to recognize and *accept* our own limitations.

b) We can take advantage of defeats to realize their *relative* character, aware that life is made up of many battles and that all is not lost by virtue of losing one particular battle.

c) Defeats help us *learn to get up* after having fallen, instead of sinking and becoming discouraged.

d) Defeats allow us to *gain experience* that will improve our work in preparation for later occasions so that we can confront challenges under more favorable conditions; they teach us what must be corrected and avoided to obtain better results.

On one occasion, Thomas Edison was asked how he had felt at the failure of so many of his attempts to produce an electric light bulb. Edison allegedly answered that he had never failed but had, in fact, successfully discovered thousands of ways in which one should not fabricate an electric light bulb. One of the clearest indicators of whether we are optimists or pessimists is how we explain our own failures. Goleman observes, "People who are optimistic see a failure as due to something that can be changed so that they can succeed next time around, while pessimists take the blame for failure, ascribing it to some lasting characteristic they are helpless to change."[18] Thus, developing optimism requires an intellectual attitude that discovers the transitory character of failures and evaluates the relative importance of the failure itself. The complement of an adequate

18. Goleman, p. 88.

explanation of the failure, if we are really optimists, would be that we *grow* instead of *resigning ourselves* in the face of negative results; that we *try once more* to attain our objectives with renewed spirits, to progress much further than we had attempted on the first try.

To conclude this chapter, I reaffirm that there is not the slightest doubt that optimism has a great influence on happiness. Being an optimist depends on a personal choice founded on hope; optimism can be considered a *feeling*, insofar as it is an emotional push that favors a positive perception of reality; it is an *attitude*, like a disposition of the will that inclines the intellect to perceive the good, and a *virtue*, if this disposition becomes something permanent and stable. Finally, optimism favors both one's relations with others and one's personal relationship with God.

5

CHAPTER

# Can Suffering Bring Happiness?

Pain and suffering are part of human life; they are inseparable from the existence of humanity,[1] although the moments of pain—their frequency and degree of intensity—can vary over time. There is also a great lack of equality among people, ranging from those who have hardly ever suffered to those whose

1. "Pain is part of being human. Anyone who really wanted to get rid of suffering would have to get rid of love before anything else, because there can be no love without suffering, because it always demands an element of self-sacrifice, because, given temperamental differences and the drama of situations, it will always bring with it renunciation and pain." Joseph Cardinal Ratzinger, *God and the World* (San Francisco: Ignatius, 2002), p. 322.

suffering has been indescribable. Is there some answer to the why of pain and the reason for these differences, or is this a mystery? Guardini, shortly before his death, said that the first thing he will do when in the presence of God is ask why men have to suffer. It seems we suffer more deeply if we do not find a satisfactory answer.

For many people, pain seems an insurmountable obstacle on the path to happiness. This is obvious for those who think that happiness is reduced to pleasure and the absence of pain (John Stuart Mill), or who feel that one has to flee from pain at all cost because it is the insurmountable enemy of happiness (Schopenhauer). However, if we consider happiness as an "interior task" that transcends pleasure and that suffering is inseparable from human life, is it possible that happiness is compatible with pain?

## Suffering and Evil

Suffering is related to evil. We suffer when we experience some evil, such as sickness, betrayal, loss of job, or the death of a child.

Evil is a certain lack or absence of a good that we expect to possess, as in the case of good health or the faithfulness of a loved one. We can say that we suffer when we lack a good in which we should or would like to participate, such as being treated with dignity or receiving recognition for exemplary professional behavior. We suffer acutely when we feel we *should* partake—in normal circumstances—of this good and yet are not able to do so, (e.g., if we are excluded from the family inheritance for no particular reason).

The evil from which pain derives can give rise to two types of suffering: *physical* and *moral.* "Physical suffering is present when 'the body is hurting' in some way, whereas moral suffering is 'pain of the soul.'"[2] Although the first may be of such intensity that it demands all of our attention, such as a bad toothache, moral suffering is ordinarily more difficult to put up with because it directly invades our state of soul and leads to internal decay, as occurs with the unexpected loss of a loved one.

2. John Paul II, *Salvifici Doloris*, 5.

Pain in itself, therefore, is not something good because it derives from evil, but it can be transformed into an important value if it is channeled adequately, if it is assigned meaning or holds the potential to have meaning. Then it ceases to be an obstacle to happiness. Even more, it can be turned into a resource that contributes to happiness. In the words of John Paul II, "joy comes from the discovery of the meaning of suffering."[3] How is this possible? What is the process that leads to this transformation?

## The Process of Suffering

The trajectory of sorrow varies from one person to another. Nonetheless, I will highlight the stages that are most frequent when suffering overcomes various kinds of natural resistance and resolves in a positive way.

**1)** It is normal that the first reaction to an unexpected, sorrowful event is one of *rejection*, of *flight*, or even of *negation*: not recognizing

3. John Paul II, *Salvifici Doloris*, 1.

it, not confronting it, or thinking that it is not real. If we do not overcome this disposition, it is impossible to channel the problem. As the fact remains present even if we try to not to see it, the artificial barrier cannot remain; sooner or later, the reality ends up imposing itself. In addition, when the reality makes its presence felt and we do not want to accept it, an interior conflict is generated, creating an imbalance and potentially leading to despair.

2) In contrast, if we overcome that first reaction and *we recognize* with realism the sorrowful fact, we have the possibility of confronting it. But this does not mean that the way is easy. The consciousness of the event can provoke an interior paralysis, collapse, or depression, any of which may prevent us from confronting what has happened and seeking some outlet or channel for our grief. If we do not overcome this state of passivity, our suffering will grow until it becomes unbearable. Until we pass this phase, it is very difficult to find or discover any meaning in the pain experienced, because our state of mind makes it difficult to comprehend.

3) In some cases, we move to an understanding of the situation only because we cannot remain in that painful state of paralysis and passivity; the negative effects that we are experiencing are harmful; therefore, we must make an effort to *overcome* the situation and react in some way. Although we may be motivated by the need to free the ego from the prison in which it finds itself, concern for others may be a positive motivation as well. For example, a mother may understand that she has to react in order to sustain her children; the head of a business is aware of obligations to employees, and so on.

4) Once we have recognized the painful event and grown ready to overcome our paralysis and passivity—although the pain and sorrow may continue eating at our hearts—ordinarily, we realize that our efforts are beginning to *pay off*. This is enough to evoke *resignation*, which is not yet an acceptance of the pain but submission to an inevitable destiny, though we do not fully identify with it.

5) Paradoxically, the realism of confronting the painful event produces a certain feeling of

dominion over the situation, which generates peace in contrast to the anxiety resulting from refusing to recognize what has happened. In addition, knowledge of the truth about a situation clarifies our thoughts and permits us to *intuit*, although perhaps still in a confused way, that *something good* can be found in what has happened or derived from it.

6) All of these stages encourage a further step, one of great importance, which pertains to the will: we begin to accept something we initially rejected and which we absolutely did not want to accept. Acceptance at this level depends on how much we benefited in recognizing and confronting the event, as well from realizing that a possible good may be derived.

7) Once we have accepted, even minimally, the painful fact, it will be possible *to ask ourselves:* Is there anything positive in all of this? What benefits can I derive from what has happened? Is it possible to take advantage of it to improve myself or to help others improve? These are questions that deal with the *meaning* of pain: *why* and *for what reason* am I suffering? The fact that we are asking

these questions is an implicit acknowledgment that there could be an answer and that if there was, the answer could be accepted.

**8)** Before attempting an answer, let us note what it means *to accept suffering*, which is the last stage of the process. Accepting is an act of the will which consists in *wanting* something that there is a reason to desire, despite the fact that it might be natural to reject it. Courage is required to overcome both that resistance and the fear of pain[4] so that the will remains free to want the good that is enclosed in the suffering. Further, one could say that true acceptance consists in *loving* what one has accepted. For this reason, true acceptance of suffering leads to valuing the suffering that presents itself as inevitable, not for itself, but insofar as it is helpful in some way. To take this definitive step, to accept suffering fully, one must understand its value and its meaning. If one succeeds in this, what Julián Marías affirms will become a reality: that

4. "*What really hurts is not so much suffering itself as the fear of suffering.* If welcomed trustingly and peacefully, suffering makes us grow." Jacques Philippe, *Interior Freedom* (New York: Scepter, 2007), p. 47.

"one can be happy—radically and substantially happy—amidst considerable bitterness, deprivation, and suffering."[5]

### The Meaning of Suffering

Questioning the *why* of suffering is a search for its cause. Is punishment due for some fault committed? Is it the consequence of bad luck? Is it because of my physical or moral weakness? Did someone intentionally cause it? Why did God permit it? The question involving the reason points to the purpose of suffering and is, therefore, related to its meaning. How can this suffering benefit me? Does it offer me an opportunity to obtain some good? What relation does it have to the purpose I have been aiming for in my life? How can I take advantage of it and use it to help others? Is it a means of bringing me closer to God?

Of course, suffering never loses its objective negativity, which, as I've said, derives from its relationship to evil. Therefore, to

5. Marías, 214.

discover the meaning of suffering, to value it and to accept it—even to love it in the most elevated degree of acceptance—does not mean to suppress the awareness of evil that it provoked. In other words, "Love of suffering does not mean the destruction of the negativity of suffering, nor to masochism, but to the discovery of a horizon in which suffering, far from destroying a person, is an instrument which transforms and perfects one";[6] it makes one "become more." Wherein does that transformation and perfection consist which suffering can produce in the one who experiences it? In other words, what is the value of suffering that makes the person *be more?*

## The Human Value of Suffering

Suffering possesses a value, human as well as spiritual; it can transform and perfect on the anthropological level of our principal human faculties—intellect, will, and

6. Antonio Malo, *Anthropología de la afectividad* (Pamplona: EUNSA, 2004), p. 179.

feelings—making us better persons, or spiritually, insofar as we get closer to God and approach the transcendent purpose of our lives. Let us begin by pointing out the human benefits we may derive from focused and accepted suffering in terms of each of the three faculties we have mentioned.

### 1) *Suffering enriches the intellect*

The activity of the intellect consists in knowing. Suffering *makes us think*; it invites us to *reflect*, to consider our lives in new ways, and to ask about the ultimate meaning of our experiences. "'One learns little from a victory but a lot from defeat,' says a Japanese proverb. Every crisis is a source of life. Every circumstance is a gift from above, especially when it leads us to experience our deficiencies and limitations, rejections and hard criticisms."[7] As a consequence, the person becomes deeper; the suffering has made him define and clarify his own convictions as well as the hierarchy of his values.

---

7. Jutta Burggraf, *Made for Freedom* (New York: Scepter, 2012), Kindle edition.

In addition, suffering allows us to *know ourselves better*, with more realism and objectivity,[8] because suffering confronts us with ourselves, without leaving space for feigning or falsehood. As a consequence of this self-knowledge, we finds ourselves in a position to show ourselves as we really are, with naturalness, because the suffering helps take off the masks and eliminate the false appearances. We may then live with more interior peace, because there is nothing to hide and we are in the presence of the truth about ourselves.

### 2) *Suffering perfects the will*

In the first place, it helps us to *accept* our own limitations and weaknesses, which emerge more openly in suffering. It often happens that those who consider themselves invulnerable, in the face of a sickness or some other painful event, must bow their heads and recognize that they are not self-sufficient, that they are not enough by themselves; they need

8. "The capacity for suffering almost defines the quality of a human being, because it brings him a consciousness of his own limitation which is a key to understanding himself." A. Llano, 80.

others. This acceptance of weakness is an act of the will that leads to *humility*, which is fundamental for being centered on life and for gaining interior peace, because "humility is truth." This humble disposition frequently leads to *solidarity* with others, recognizing a reciprocal need. This relationship of mutual aid has a direct influence on happiness, because sharing is indispensable to being happy.

In addition, when we are capable of overcoming the depressing effect of suffering and, instead of sinking, overcome it and move ahead, we are *strengthened*. Therefore, suffering is a school of strength, because it offers us the opportunity to learn to support the adverse and develop a strength of will capable of confronting hard situations that may come in the future and which might otherwise produce fear or propel us to reject them flatly. The strength we acquire in suffering is a key factor for our happiness because it allows us to overcome adversities that we meet in life and carry out our objectives; doing so is an accomplishment on which depends, in good measure, our happiness. In contrast, those who lack strength of will usually go from frustration to frustration, accumulating bitterness because they do not succeed in carrying out what they propose.

### 3) *Suffering transforms the heart*

The primordial importance of love in relation to happiness is obvious to a certain extent, since it is not difficult to see that "people who really and truly love each other are the happiest people in the world."[9] It is important remember that the capacity to love comes from having been loved previously. For example, a child learns to love to the extent that he has experienced the love of his parents. Happiness comes from love, because "the desire of being loved is essential to happiness; when someone loves us, our life expands; it literally opens to the possibility of being happy."[10]

Nevertheless, to experience the love of others is not enough to be happy; it is also necessary to *know ourselves* and *feel ourselves loved*. When we know ourselves and feel

---

9. Teresa of Calcutta, *No Greater Love*, (Novato, CA: New World Library, 1997), p. 131.

10. Marías, p. 293.

ourselves confirmed by love, we notice a kind of impulse toward our own plenitude, for as Pieper points out, "Only through a *confirmation in love* which comes from another does the human being live at all."[11] In other words, "When a man *feels himself loved*, his existential landscape is lit up and his life begins to turn around this light."[12] With this experience, the capacity to love expands, because it blossoms from a desire to correspond to the love received. In living out this desire, we experience happiness with special intensity, as a consequence of feeling ourselves loved and of loving. What we can conclude from this is of capital importance: that "the essence of happiness is simple and eternal: it consists in loving and being loved."[13]

Now we find that true love of others becomes more powerful with suffering. Pain that is accepted is an antidote to egoism and an opening towards the other. In the end, even the 'yes' to love is a source of suffering,

11. Pieper, *El amor* (Madrid: Rialp 1972), p. 58.

12. Martí, Miguel-Ángel, *La ilusión*, (Pamplona: EUNSA, 1995), pp. 37–38.

13. Poupard, p. 149. I

because love always requires expropriations of my 'I,' in which I allow myself to be pruned and wounded. Love simply cannot exist without this painful renunciation of myself, for otherwise it becomes pure selfishness and thereby ceases to be love."[14]

This love, born of suffering, is shown especially in *understanding* of others. When we gain a clearer consciousness of our limitations, we become more capable of really putting ourselves in the shoes of others in order to understand them and accept them as they are. In addition, the experience of pain makes us more sensitive to the suffering of others, whom we understand more deeply. We who gain in understanding are generally more *cordial*, more *kind*, and more *friendly*, all qualities of great importance for living with others and for personal perfection, and which contribute decisively to happiness. In light of these consequences for love, which are derived from suffering, we can say with the poet, "I don't want you to go, / pain, last

14. Joseph Ratzinger as quoted in Girhard Lohfink, *No Irrelevant Jesus: On Jesus and the Church Today*, trans. Linda M. Maloney (Collegeville, MN: Liturgical Press, 2014), p. 101.

form / of loving. I feel myself / live when you hurt me . . ."[15]

The benefits derived from suffering in each of these three faculties that I have pointed out lead to true *maturity* and *plenitude* because they open our eyes to the transcendence of life, to the need of using our freedom well and of living with a sense of responsibility. It is not unusual to find that those who formerly lived an easy and superficial life, marked by mediocrity and conformism, have been transformed by an experience of suffering. They began to ask themselves the reason for their existence; they recognized the time lost prior to that moment; they concluded that it was not worthwhile to live in that way and decided to take themselves seriously in the future.

Thus an event that is difficult to cope with, such as a serious sickness, "can also make a person more mature, helping him discern in his life what is not essential so that he can turn toward that which is."[16] When this

15. Pedro Salinas, *Love Poems by Pedro Salinas: My Voice Because of You*, trans. Willis Barnstone (Chicago: The University of Chicago Press, 2010), p. 115.

16. *CCC*, 1501.

transformation translates into an eagerness to give the best of ourselves, to employ our abilities and strengths to make them render as much as possible, and is oriented also to the service of others, we are then moving toward fullness, and the experience of happiness will not be long in coming.

## The Spiritual Value of Suffering

These human reasons certainly allow us to find a meaning in suffering that helps us on the path to happiness. Nevertheless, we also have to recognize that such reasons are not sufficient for helping us to discover the final and transcendent meaning of pain and to resolve the problem of happiness in a definitive way. It is a matter of experience that those who do not believe in God and in life after death do not find happiness because that absence produces an interior emptiness that translates into loneliness, anxiety, and bitterness. The aspirations for infinity that they experience in their hearts find no channel or answer; the meaning of life is also frustrated before the constant menace of death and the consciousness of the fleetingness of all things. Their suffering can be seen as pure negativity because they are unable to discover its transcendent value; thus suffering becomes an insoluble obstacle to happiness.

The research on happiness by David Myers and Ed Diener (cited earlier) produced the significant conclusion that religiously active people report greater happiness, findings reinforced by related studies revealing that "reported happiness and life satisfaction rise with strength of religious affiliation and frequency of attendance at worship services.[17] This conclusion was also supported by a Gallup study that compared the happiness levels of those who had a "low spiritual commitment" versus those who had "high spirituality."[18]

The chaplains of a university hospital confirmed that "there are people who have everything and are not happy; nevertheless

---

17. Myers and Diener, p. 56.

18. The Gallup survey consulted a cross-section of Americans, comparing those low in "spiritual commitment" with highly religious people. Their finding was that "highly religious people were twice as likely as those lowest in spiritual commitment to declare themselves 'very happy.'" Myers and Diener, p. 56.

it is not difficult to find sick people who, with great joy, give thanks to God for the marvelous world that they have discovered thanks to their sickness."[19] These experiential discoveries confirm the affirmation of St. Augustine that "those who possess God are happy."[20] In all of these cases, spirituality is not only compatible with suffering but is also capable of turning pain into a source of happiness because of the relationship that the person has with God. In what does this relationship consist?

The answer could be summed up in the theological virtues of *faith*, *hope*, and *charity*, which, according to the *Catechism of the Catholic Church*, "dispose Christians to live in a relationship with the Holy Trinity. . . . They are infused by God into the souls of the faithful to make them capable of acting as his children and of meriting eternal life."[21] This means that "we do not exist in order to pursue just any happiness. We have been called

19. Miguel Ángel Monge and José Luis León, *El sentido del sufrimiento* (Madrid: Ediciones Palabra 2001), p. 16.

20. Augustine, *On the Happy Life* 2.12.

21. *CCC*, 1812 and 1813.

to penetrate the intimacy of God's own life, to know and love God the Father, God the Son, and God the Holy Spirit."[22] We will see later how each of these virtues influences happiness, to what degree suffering can give us power and thus help us to be happier, and how these virtues also convert suffering into a path of happiness.

### 1) *Faith*

Faith is a virtue by which we believe in God and believe God. To *believe in* God means to recognize the existence of a creating being, infinitely good and powerful, in whom we can trust and on whom we can count at every moment. By faith, we center our lives on God and make an effort to know and do his will. We see God as a loving father and experience, by consequence, the certainty of a child who is confident of being protected and accompanied at every moment. This trust has a direct repercussion on our happiness because of the consequent tranquility and interior peace that we experience.

---

22. Escrivá, *Christ Is Passing By*, 133.

To *believe* God means to accept all that he has revealed to us. Our definitive happiness consists in union with God forever in the next life. Among other things, the truths that orient our lives toward that definitive happiness also point out the path that it is necessary to follow—for example, the fulfillment of the commandments—in order to attain this goal. Faith assures us that one who lives in accord with God's plan will attain happiness, not only in the next life, but also in this one, although with the limitations proper to one who is still underway. In this way, our happiness on earth is like a prelude to the definitive happiness in heaven. Faith, therefore, gives us such clarity about the ultimate truths of life that life is illuminated and full of meaning, with the consequent joy and happiness that derive from this.

As I've noted, suffering puts us in contact with our defects and permits us to realize our ontological limitations. It offers us in this same measure the possibility of discovering or becoming conscious of our *dependence on God.* Victor Hugo said, "To discern God, the eye often needs the lens of tears," which opens us up to faith. Pain ordinarily overturns attitudes of self-sufficiency—pride, self-love—which make faith difficult, because they prevent us from recognizing the need for God in our own lives. "Very often illness provokes a search for God and a return to him."[23]

The following testimony is significant in this respect. "Only the crucible of anguish permitted my faith to be multiplied and purified. Including, curiously, that I experienced this in its effects: now when I speak of Christ, people believe in what I say more, because now I know very well that what I am saying is not nonsense."[24] Many saints opened up to the faith and made the decision to turn toward God precisely because of a sad event; they were thus transformed and began on the path that led them to full happiness.

On the other hand, faith permits us to discover the meaning of suffering, even in those situations in which we turn to God to solve a problem, such as physical pain or sickness, when we don't receive the hoped-for

23. *CCC*, 1501.

24. Martin Descalzo, quoted in Monge and León, p. 92.

response. Robert Spaemann explains this on the basis of a specific experience:

> I was able to be a witness in Lourdes of a sick person who was cured, as happens from time to time in Lourdes, in a manner incomprehensible to the doctors. But it was not the cure that made the deepest impression on me, but the sick people who went to Lourdes without having been cured. One might suppose that they would be filled with the deepest despair, but far from it! Just the contrary! The greatest miracle at Lourdes is the serenity of those who leave there without being cured. How could this happen? The reality is related to the fact that the miraculous cure of a few makes them understand that the suffering that they are undergoing is not a fatal destiny. If God could cure me, he must have a reason for not doing so. A motive, that is to say, a meaning, and a meaning gives one consolation.[25]

---

25. Spaemann, Robert, "El sentido del sufrimiento," Universidad de Navarra, *http://www.unav.es/capellaniauniversitaria.*

### 2) *Hope*

Hope is the virtue by which we aspire to definitive union with God in eternal life. It includes putting our trust in the promises that he has made and in the means by which he has promised we will attain it. "The virtue of hope responds to the aspiration to happiness which God has placed in the heart of every man."[26]

It is not difficult to understand, therefore, the close relationship that this theological virtue has with happiness. Hope for the future gives meaning to life, generates enthusiasm, and moves us to draw upon all our potentialities to reach the goal. Our present happiness depends on perceiving the future positively, with the possibility of being more and more happy, as the contrary would produce within us a constriction of spirit that would turn into sadness—our expectations of the future would be confused or frustrated in advance. But in order to see the future as being more and more happy, we need to be convinced that someday, we can be happy in a full and definitive sense, because man feels happy

---

26. *CCC*, 1818.

to the extent of the reasonable hope that he entertains of attaining true happiness. This conviction is possible only if we have hope, if we experience the security of knowing that because we live in conformity with the will of God, at the end of life on earth, we will reach the definitive meeting with him, the only source of absolute happiness.

When suffering appears, it can become an obstacle to happiness. But it can also provoke us to ask ourselves: if God wants us to be happy now—within the limits proper to the human condition—and happy in the next life, has he specified the way of attaining that goal in the midst of suffering? The answer can be found in Jesus, who pointed out the way in the Beatitudes that he taught us on the Sermon on the Mount.[27] Let us recall some of them that focus on suffering, written down by St. Matthew:

> Blessed are those who mourn, for they shall be comforted.
>
> Blessed are those who hunger and thirst for righteousness, for they shall be satisfied.

27. See Mt 5:3–12 and Lk 6:20–26.

> Blessed are those who are persecuted for righteousness' sake, for theirs is the kingdom of heaven.
>
> Blessed are you when men revile you and persecute you and utter all kinds of evil against you falsely on my account. Rejoice and be glad, for your reward is great in heaven.[28]

With the Beatitudes, Jesus provided divine instruction for happiness, each directive paired with a promise. Hence "the Beatitudes of the Gospel cause us to meet, beneath the moving sand of intermittent joys and deceptive pleasures, the path of our true happiness."[29] Its knowledge will be a light that orients the path of that deep happiness for which we all long.

### *3) Love*

Charity, *love,* is the virtue by which we love God and love our neighbor. As discussed, the capacity to love comes from having been loved first. This is especially true on the ontological

28. See Mt 5: 4, 6, 10–12.

29. Chevrot, pp. 29–30.

and radical level, where the point of departure is in God, as Benedict XVI noted: "He has loved us first and he continues to do so; we too, then, can respond with love."[30] Therefore, the person who knows himself to be loved by God experiences the "joy in God that becomes his essential happiness,"[31] and one who corresponds to that love feels happy, because "our happiness lies in abiding in the love that made us and gives us life."[32]

But there is an obstacle to the love of God and of our neighbor, with consequences for our happiness: it is *sin*, which consists in voluntarily transgressing the order that God has established for our good, to make our way easier. Sin separates us from God; it stains us interiorly and merits punishment for the fault committed. This is why the subjective effect of personal faults is experienced as a weight

30. Benedict XVI, *Deus Caritas Est*, Encyclical Letter, December 25, 2005, 17, Vatican website: *http://w2.vatican.va/content/benedict-xvi/en/encyclicals/documents/hf_ben-xvi_enc_20051225_deus-caritas-est.html*.

31. Benedict XVI, *Deus Caritas Est*, 9.

32. John Paul II, as quoted in Paul J. Wadell *Happiness and the Christian Moral Life: An Introduction to Christian Ethics*, 2nd ed. (New York: Rowman & Littlefield, 2012), p. 11.

on the conscience in the form of remorse, which takes away interior peace. How is it possible to repair what we have lost by sinning? Among other means, suffering offered to God can be converted into a privileged pathway to pay the debt contracted, to purify the soul from the stains that have come from those offenses to God, and to recuperate the good that has been lost through distancing ourselves from him. John Paul II explained that suffering "has a meaning not only because it serves to repay the objective evil of the transgression with another evil, but first and foremost because it creates the possibility of rebuilding goodness in the subject who suffers. This is an extremely important aspect of suffering."[33] In other words, "the soul shattered by pain is cleansed from the stain of guilt and recovers its former beauty and its former vigor."[34] It is not difficult to show that the subjective effect of this reparation is deep interior happiness. This is why St. Josemaría said: "When we advance beyond the stage

33. John Paul II, *Salvifici Doloris*, 12.

34. Antonio Royo Marín, *Nada te turbe, nada te espante* (Mexico City: MiNos, 1998), p. 22.

of simply tolerating difficulties or sufferings (whether physical or moral) and, instead, love them and offer them to God in reparation for our sins and the sins of all mankind, then, I assure you, they do not distress us."[35]

Suffering is additionally a privileged way of demonstrating and showing love. The best example is found in Jesus Christ, who experienced physical and moral pain to an unspeakable degree, especially in the moments of his Passion, in order to save mankind. One could say that the mystery of pain is illuminated by and can be understood deeply only from the Cross of Christ.[36] It is a mystery of love; the mystery of a God whose love is so great that he became man and gave his life for us. Christ suffered in place of man and for man. And every man, by means of his own suffering, can make himself a participant in the redemptive suffering of Christ, which does not end in the Cross, but in the joy of the Resurrection.

---

35. Escrivá, *Friends of God*, 132.

36. "Christ, and more specifically Christ crucified, is the only one who gives true meaning to pain and sickness, to life and to death. Without him, the consideration of those realities remains impoverished, because in addition they become mysterious and disconcerting." Monge and León, p. 205.

Therefore, love of neighbor can be shown in an effective way by means of suffering. If it is offered to God for others, it becomes a prayer of incalculable value because a person who is capable of praying for another through his own suffering is demonstrating a love that is generous, as was that of Jesus, and is uniting his suffering to that of Christ with a consequent benefit for that other person. "By his own passion and death, he gave new meaning to our suffering which, when united with his own, can become a means of purification and of salvation for us and for others."[37] If any service carried out for one's neighbor usually brings with it an increase of happiness in the one who carries it out, if the help is directed to the most important aspect of the person—his or her relationship with God—one can understand that the happiness derived therefrom will reach an especially high level. Thus, it is not strange that St. Paul stated, "I rejoice in my sufferings for your sake."[38]

---

37. *Compendium of the Catechism of the Catholic Church*, 314.
38. Col 1:24.

# Conclusion

After these reflections, we can conclude that suffering—which is in itself an evil—can be converted into a good, leading us to a fullness of happiness. Not only can suffering *not* be an obstacle to happiness but also it can be compatible with and even strengthen it. This will certainly be true only after a serious and well-oriented effort, but with our love and trust placed in God, from whom comes our principal help, pain and suffering can be turned into a source of happiness. This last is possible when we have centered our lives on God, as is expressed in the following verses of a poet of the twentieth century:

> I do not want my suffering to be
> Visible in my singing;
> I want to suffer and be silent,

I don't want to give people
Crumbs of my suffering . . .

You alone, my God and Lord,
You who wound me out of love;
You, who with immense love,
Try with greater pain
The souls you love the most.

You alone have to know,
For I only want to tell of
My secret suffering,
To the one who has to understand
And who is able to console.

Blessed are you Lord,
For your infinite goodness,
Because you lovingly place,
On the thorns of sorrow,
Roses of conformity."[1]

1. José María Pemán, *Obras Completas*, Tomo 1, *Poesía*, (Madrid: Escelicer S. L., 1947), pp. 149–150.

# Appendix

## Features of a Mature Personality

The reflections developed throughout these pages presuppose a condition that, to the extent that it is fulfilled, makes happiness possible: that the subject has a mature and psychologically sound personality. Features that characterize this personality include the following:

1) *Knowing myself,* both in what refers to my own temperament and character as well as the principal strengths and weaknesses I possess. This self-knowledge must be realistic, objective, and not deformed by my own subjectivity, and it requires a capacity for reflection and self-criticism.

2) *Accepting myself,* which implies digesting the past, identifying myself with the present, and having clarity with regard to the

future.[1] Acceptance favors security, which is also a characteristic of a mature personality and which permits me to develop with naturalness and simplicity, without affectations or artificial poses.

3) *Adapting to my surroundings,* which consists in having a friendly relationship with my exterior reality and in not becoming involved in frequent conflicts.

4) *Possessing consistency,* a congruence between what I think and what I do, with my thoughts anchored in the truth about myself.

5) *Experiencing a harmonious integration between my intellect, my will, and my emotions,*[2] where each faculty carries out what corresponds to it: "a cool head, arms of steel, a heart of fire," said Balmes. In this consists psychological

1. A detailed analysis on the operations of *knowing oneself* and *accepting oneself,* in order to be authentic, can be found in Francisco Ugarte, *En busca de la realidad* (Madrid: Rialp, 2006), pp. 110–116.

2. "The development of character, first of all, seeks a harmonious and integrated relationship between these three principal aspects of the reality of man: the intellect, the will, and the feelings." Carlos Llano, *Formación de la inteligencia, la voluntad y el carácter* (Mexico City: Trillas, 1999), p. 116.

maturity,[3] which involves emotional stability,[4] often difficult to attain.

6) *Exhibiting autonomy and responsibility,* which is the capacity to decide for myself, to make good use of personal freedom, to favor creativity, and to account for my own acts, with ethical criteria.

7) *Proposing for myself worthwhile goals*—derived from a broad life vision—which implies challenges and generates enthusiasm and drive so that life is full of meaning, I live with intensity, and my potentialities develop as much as possible.

8) *Working to my potential.* Work done well is an irreplaceable resource for personal development; and, in the supernatural order, it is a fundamental means of sanctification.[5]

---

3. Psychological maturity is the "capacity to submit all of our impulses, desires, and emotions to the direction of our will." Aquilino Polaino-Lorente, *Madurez personal y amor conyugal* (Madrid: Rialp, 1995), p. 10.

4. See Beatriz Quintanilla, *Personalidad madura* (Mexico City: Publicaciones Cruz O., 2003), p. 120.

5. "*Sanctifying work is to sanctify the human activity of working;* all the rest are immediate consequences: from the sanctification of the person who is working to the sanctification of the structures of the world of men and women." Fernando Ocáriz, *Naturaleza, gracia y gloria* (Pamplona: EUNSA, 2000), 267.

It requires order and constancy to realize, at each moment, what is necessary (with a hierarchy of values) and to be able to reach the end of the road.

9) *Living with gratitude* contributes to valuing the gifts I have received and downplaying the importance of grievances—real or imaginary—proceeding from others or from circumstances. It helps to avoid three direct enemies of happiness: a sense of victimization (proper to those who feel injured by everything and everyone), resentment, and envy.

10) *Enjoying friendship*[6] *and an adequate social life,* where I can live out the love and affection that I give and receive.

11) *Maintaining a sense of humor,* which permits me to laugh, even at myself, and which constantly increases my personal joy and that of those around me.

12) *Orienting my life toward God and toward others,* in place of egoistically centering it on myself.

---

6. "Anyone who is to be happy, then, will need virtuous friends." Aristotle, *Nicomachean Ethics*, 9.9, as translated in Crisp, p. 179.

# Works Cited


Ardoin, Paul, S. E. Gontarski, and Laci Mattison, eds. *Understanding Bergson, Understanding Modernism.* New York: Bloomsbury, 2013.

Aristotle. *Nicomachean Ethics.* Translated by Roger Crisp. UK: Cambridge University Press, 2000.

Aquinas, Thomas. *De Potentia* 10.2.5 in *The Power of God.* Translated by Richard J. Regan. Oxford, NY: Oxford University Press, 2012.

———. Summa Theologica 1–2 and 2–2.

Augustine of Hippo. *Expositions on the Psalms, Vol. V.*

———. *On the Happy Life.*

Benedict XVI. *Deus Caritas Est.* Encyclical. December 25, 2005. Vatican website: *http://w2.vatican.va/content/benedict-xvi/en/encyclicals/documents/hf_ben-xvi_enc_20051225_deus-caritas-est.html.*

Borges, Jorge Luis. "Remorse." Translated by Willis Barnstone in *Six Masters of the Spanish Sonnet.* Carbondale, IL: Southern Illinois University Press, 1993.

Burggraf, Jutta. *Made for Freedom.* New York: Scepter, 2012. Kindle edition.

*Catechism of the Catholic Church* (2nd ed.), Washington, DC: Libreria Editrice Vaticana–United States Conference of Catholic Bishops, 2000.

*Compendium of the Catechism of the Catholic Church*, Washington, DC: Libreria Editrice Vaticana–United States Conference of Catholic Bishops, 2006.

Chevrot, Georges. *Las Bienaventuranzas*. Madrid: Rialp, 1987.

Chrysostom, John. Homilies on Romans.

Covey, Stephen R. *The 7 Habits of Highly Effective People*. New York: Free Press, 1994.

de Cervantes, Miguel. *Complete Works of Miguel de Cervantes*. Translated by John Ormsby. UK: Delphi Classics, 2013. Digital version.

Descalzo, José Luis Martín. *Razones para la alegria*. Madrid: Sociedad de Educación Atenas, 1998.

Dmitri Royster, *The Kingdom of God: The Sermon on the Mount* (Crestwood, NY: St. Vladimir's Seminary Press, 1992.

Echevarría, Javier. *Getsemaní*. Barcelona: Planeta, 2005.

Escrivá, Josemaría. *Friends of God*. New York: Scepter, 2002.

———. *Christ Is Passing By*. New York: Scepter, 2002.

———. *The Forge*. New York: Scepter, 2011.

———. *The Way / The Furrow / The Forge*. New York: Scepter, 2011.

Farrell, Walter, and Martin J. Healy. *My Way of Life: The Summa Simplified for Everyone*. Brooklyn: Confraternity of the Precious Blood, 1952.

Frankl, Viktor. *Psicoanálisis y existencialismo*. Mexico City: Fondo de Cultura Económica, 1967.

Fredrick, David, ed. *The Roman Gaze: Vision, Power, and the Body*. Baltimore: The Johns Hopkins University Press, 2002.

Garcia Hoz, Víctor. *Pedagogía de la lucha ascética*. Madrid: Rialp, 1963.

Goleman, Daniel. *Emotional Intelligence*. New York: Bantam, 1997.

John Paul II. *Salvifici Doloris*. Apostolic Letter. February 11, 1984. Vatican website: *https://w2.vatican.va/content/john-paul-ii/en/apost_letters/1984/documents/hf_jp-ii_apl_11021984_salvifici-doloris.html.*

Layard, Richard. *La felicidad, Lecciones de una nueva ciencia*. Mexico City: Taurus, 2005.

Lewis, C. S. *Surprised by Joy: The Shape of My Early Life*. Orlando: Harcourt Brace & Co, 1955.

Llano, Alejandro. *La vida lograda*. Barcelona: Ariel, 2002.

Llano, Carlos. *Formación de la intelligencia, la voluntad y el character.* Mexico City: Trillas, 1999.

Llano, Rafael. *Optimismo*. Mexico City: MiNos, 1994.

Lohfink, Gerhard. *No Irrelevant Jesus: On Jesus and the Church Today.* Translated by Linda M. Maloney. Collegeville, MN: Liturgical Press, 2014.

Magee, Bryan. *The Philosophy of Schopenhauer*. New York: Oxford University Press, 1983.

Malo, Antonio. *Anthropología de la afectividad*. Pamplona: Eunsa, 2004.

Marañón, Gregorio. *Tiberio: Historía de un resentimiento*. Madrid: Espasa-Calpe, 1981.

Marías, Julian. *La Felicidad humana*. Madrid: Alianza Editorial, 2005.

Marina, José Antonio. *El laberinto sentimental.* Barcelona: Anagrama, 1997.

Miguel-Ángel, Martí. *La illusion.* Pamplona, Eunsa, 1995.

Melendo, Tomás. *El "efecto" felicidad.* Mexico City: Trillas, 2008.

Mill, John Stuart. *Utilitarianism, 2nd ed.*. Edited by George Sher. Indianapolis: Hackett, 2001.

Monge, Miguel Angel and José Luis León. *El sentido del sufrimiento*. Madrid: Ediciones Palabra, 2001.

Myers, David G. *The Pursuit of Happiness.* New York: Quill, 2002.

Myers, David G. and Ed Diener. "The Pursuit of Happiness." *Scientific American*. May 1996.

Nicol, Eduardo. *Las ideas y los dias.* Mexico City: Afínita, 2007.

Niven, David. *The 100 Simple Secrets of Happy People.* San Francisco: Harper, 2000.

Ocáriz, Fernando. *Naturaleza, gracia y gloria.* Pamplona: Eunsa, 2000.

Pascal, Blaise. "Morality And Doctrine." *Pensées.* Translated by W. F. Trotter. Mineola, NY: Dover, 2003.

Paul VI. *Gaudium et spes*. Pastoral Constitution on the Church in the Modern World. December 7, 1965, 24.3, Vatican website: *http://www.vatican.va/archive/hist_councils/ii_vatican_council/documents/vat-ii_const_19651207_gaudium-et-spes_en.html.*

Paz, Octavio. *The Double Flame: Love and Eroticism.* Translated by Helen Lane. New York: Harcourt Brace & Company, 1995.

Péman, José María. Obras Completas, Tomo 1, Poesía. Madrid: Escelicer, S. L., 1947.

Peñalosa, Joaquin. *El mexicano y los 7 pecados capitales.* Mexico City: Paulinas, 1985.

Philippe, Jacques. *Interior Freedom.* New York: Scepter, 2007.

Pieper, Joseph. *El amor.* Madrid: Rialp, 1972.

Polaino-Lorente, Aquilino. *Madurez personal y amor conyugal.* Madrid: Rialp, 1995.

Polo, Leonardo. *Quién es el hombre.* Madrid: Rialp, 1998.

Poupard, Paul. Felicidad y fe cristiana. Barcelona: Herder, 1992.

Powell, John. *Happiness is an Inside Job.* Allen, TX: Tabor, 1989.

Quintanilla, Beatriz. *Personalidad madura.* Mexico City: Publicaciones Cruz O., 2003.

Ratzinger, Joseph. *God and the World.* San Francisco: Ignatius, 2002.

———. *Mirar a Cristo.* Valencia: EDICEP, 1990.

———. *Palabra en la Iglesia.* Salamanca: Sigueme, 1976.

Reale, Giovanni. *La sabiduria antigua.* Barcelona: Herder, 1996.

Rojas, Enrique. *Una teoría de la felicidad.* Madrid: Dossat 2000.

Royo Marín, Antonio. *Nada te turbe, nada te espante.* Mexico City: MiNos, 1998.

Russell, Bertrand. *The Conquest of Happiness.* Oxfordshire: Routledge Classics, 2006.

Salinas, Pedro. *Love Poems by Pedro Salinas: My Voice Because of You*. Translated by Willis Barnstone. Chicago: The University of Chicago Press, 2010.

Savater, Fernando. "Prólogo," in Russell Bertrand's *La conquista de la felicidad*. Barcelona: Debolsillo, 2004.

Scheler, Max. *Ressentiment*. Wisconsin: Marquette University Press, 1994.

Schopenhauer, Arthur. *The Basis of Morality*, 2nd ed. Translated by A.B. Bullock. New York: Dover Publications, Inc., 2005.

Second Vatican Council. Pastoral Constitution on the Church in the Modern World. *Gaudium et spes*. December 7, 1965. Vatican website: *http://www.vatican.va/archive/hist_councils/ii_vatican_council/documents/vat-ii_const_19651207_gaudium-et-spes_en.html*.

Seligman, Martin E. P. *Authentic Happiness*. Toronto: The Free Press, 2002.

Seneca. *Minor Dialogues: Together with the Dialogue on Clemency*. Translated by Aubrey Stewart. London: George Bell and Sons, 1898.

Spaemann, Robert. "El sentido del sufrimiento," Universidad de Navarra, *http://www.unav.es/servicio/capellaniauniversitaria/documentos*.

———. *Happiness and Benevolence*. Trans. J. Alberg. Edinburgh: T & T Clark, 2000.

Teresa of Calcutta. *No Greater Love*. Novato, CA: New World Library, 1997.

Ugarte, Francisco. *From Resentment to Forgiveness: A Gateway to Happiness*. New Jersey: Scepter Publishers, 2008.

———. *En busca de la realidad* (Madrid: Rialp, 2006).

Wadell, Paul J. *Happiness and the Christian Moral Life: An Introduction to Christian Ethics*, 2nd edition. New York: Rowman & Littlefield, 2012.

Witchel, Alex. "At Lunch with Malachy McCourt: How a Rogue Turns Himself into a Saint." *New York Times*, July 29, 1998.

Yepes Stork, Ricardo. *Fundamentos de antropologia.* Pamplona: EUNSA, 1996.